THE QUALITY CLASSROOM MANAGER

An Interpretation and Application of
Dr. W. Edwards Deming's
Management Philosophy Applied to
Classroom Teaching

Foreword by
Dr. William Glasser

T0347340

THE QUALITY CLASSROOM MANAGER

Bob Norton
University of Wisconsin—La Crosse

Routledge
Taylor & Francis Group
LONDON AND NEW YORK

First published 1995 Baywood Publishing Company, Inc.

2 Park Square, Milton Park, Abingdon, Oxfordshire OX14 4RN
52 Vanderbilt Avenue, New York, NY 10017

Routledge is an imprint of the Taylor & Francis Group, an informa business

First issued in paperback 2018

Library of Congress Catalog Number: 95-22715

Library of Congress Cataloging-in-Publication-Data

Main entry under title:

Norton, Robert C.
  The quality classroom manager / by Bob Norton.
    p.   cm.
  Includes bibliographical references (p.   ).
  ISBN 0-89503-131-0
  1. Classroom management.   I. Title.
  LB3013.N67 1995
  371.1'024- -dc20   95-22715
                                                      CIP

ISBN 13: 978-0-89503-131-0 (hbk)
ISBN 13: 978-0-415-78473-3 (pbk)

Contents

Foreword

All classroom teachers who are interested in investigating or developing quality classroom management techniques will find this book very helpful. Bob has skillfully written a book that will assist classroom teachers to become more understanding of students' social and learning needs and offer proven ideas of how to manage the classroom to optimize learning.

The book is based upon his thirty-two years of public school work, the principles of control theory/reality therapy and ideas taken from Dr. William Deming's quality management program. The blending of these three is what makes the book become theoretically correct and very practical.

When reading a book, it is relatively easy to discover if the material is authentic. It is obvious that this book is built upon practical classroom experiences. Bob has used his past and present school-based experiences, as well as consulted with many teachers and learners to develop the ideas for a quality classroom manager. This input from students and teachers is a prime factor that causes authenticity. An example of this fact is in Chapter 2, when he verifies the painful truth that few students relate quality to classroom experiences, then uses the students' perception that extra-curricular involvement does often equate into quality and follows up with classroom teachers' conclusions of why this is true. The sixteen conclusions that are identified become the challenge of quality classroom management.

Dr. Deming believed, as well as I, that in order for quality to become a reality, the barriers of differences, competition that is counterproductive to teaching, assigned and/or assumed power and coercion must be removed. Bob has addressed these barriers, and his work with teachers to expand their classroom management repertoire to include the seven grouping patterns that are explained in Chapter 3 goes a long way in breaking down the student-to-student barriers that are present in individually student managed classrooms.

The chapter on teacher-parent partnershipping addresses the need as well as a basic plan on how to break down the barriers that inhibit the partnership. It is obvious that the teacher-parent partnership has to be developed and the first step is realizing that parents must become equal team members in education of their child. The plan to identify areas of responsibility of principal guidance team, classroom teacher, and student and/or parent involvement is an important aspect of quality education.

Chapter 4, focusing on techniques to teach students the process of learning self-assessors, is well developed. It does a good job of explaining the reasons students need to have the skills of self-assessment and offers a working model of how to teach the skills.

The book is accurately and practically written and is a definite contribution to quality management of classroom teachers.

Dr. William Glasser

1

Introduction

The reason for writing this book is to assist classroom teachers in their continual quest of becoming quality teachers. The quest is truly continual because what constitutes a quality classroom teacher is the fact that he/she is continually improving his/her performance by updating, experimenting, discussing, and perfecting improved techniques. This book is designed to build an understanding of what constitutes quality classroom management, why there is a need to focus on quality and have it become the basic outcome of student performance in both social and academic learning, and how to incorporate quality learning as part of the everyday classroom experience.

I feel confident to embark upon the adventure of writing a book based upon the experiences that thirty-two years of public school work have provided. During my tenure I have had the opportunity to study, observe, participate and think as I attempt to understand how effective teachers have assisted students to become effective learners. The majority of the observations and study has resulted from my personal managing and teaching experiences, which include five years of elementary classroom teaching, five years of principalships, two years of elementary, three years of middle school, two years of curriculum coordination, two years as school psychologist and director of special education and eighteen years teaching at the university level. I believe that each of the thirty-two years constitute legitimate experience as the positions gave me the opportunity to continually develop management techniques as I attempted to persuade individuals to grow, adapt, and at times follow procedure. Public school work fell primarily into the managing category as the job usually involved the need to moderate or attempt to convince someone to do something.

My opportunity to teach came about due to my having the privilege to teach graduate students. The students were self-motivated, self-directed, knew what they wanted and focused on expanding their knowledge base or perfection of skills, were never a discipline problem and were always interested in creating quality products. Teaching is fun, and easy, when you have students that want to learn and I have been fortunate to have had such students.

Public and private school teachers seldom have the opportunity to "just" teach as they have to spend the majority of their time managing. They must motivate, plan, discipline, direct, re-direct, re-teach, evaluate, report, supervise, and seldom find the time to just teach.

The following chapters focus on managing techniques that I believe will build the foundation for a quality managed classroom, resulting in increased academic and social learning outcomes. As I have studied quality to provide leadership for quality classroom management, I have realized how past thinking and educational practices have been extremely detrimental to quality teaching. There are two distinct points where quality teaching can be evaluated: products and relationships. The traditional individualized classroom, with its emphasis on factual knowledge and self-learning, has focused the evaluation process to product evaluation and programmed the thinking about educational outcomes to be perceived as individual knowledge gained and test scores quantified. This prevalent thought has then been used by the political manipulators to convince the general public that quality teaching can be test score validated. Universities have fallen for the same trap as they base entry qualifications on test scores and grade point averages.

The basic concept of quantified quality teaching through individual student product evaluation is no longer valid. The worker of the twenty-first century is no longer a single producer working in an isolated environment. The worker is a member of a team, that builds upon the talents and knowledge of each other, and through the use of collaboration, develops quality products.

What now constitutes quality teaching is the ability of the classroom teacher to develop classroom relationships that foster the collaboration. Quality is the result of teachers who become managers who have the knowledge and skills to create an environment and provide the training for the students, who are the workers, to positively relate, create, problem solve, and self-evaluate the quality of their work. The final products they develop must be of a level quality, and are a result of quality management built around relationship management skills.

This is a major shift in understanding as teachers are trained to be product oriented, with minimal training in relationships management.

Teacher training institutions must proceed with major overhauling and begin training the teachers of the twenty-first century to first of all understand the shift, and then provide the necessary training for the perfection of relationships management.

The following six chapters focus on management techniques that will build the foundation for a quality managed classroom that will increase academic and social learning outcomes. With each of the six management techniques are vision statements as anticipated outcomes.

1. Quality becomes a means to develop definition and purpose for self-evaluation.
   a. The teachers and students will perceive self and others as valuable, talented individuals with desire and ability to do quality work.
   b. Quality work and quality produced products will increase pride in work and self and the process will become self-motivating.
   c. Quality will become the basic component for evaluating the learning environment, the process to produce products, the products, and the interpersonal connections that are inherent in quality relationship management.
   d. Quality is a personal statement that reflects individual's present knowledge, beliefs, and values and is in constant flux and definition.
2. Connectiveness as it relates to teacher/student relationships, student to student relationships, and relevancy of learning.
   a. There is continuous opportunity for personal one-to-one communication and relating between the teacher and the individual students.
   b. Students continuously experience a learning environment that depicts the value, excitement, and high quality of work that group learning produces.
   c. Students experience and value the individual differences that each brings to the learning experience.
   d. Students understand and experience the fact that diversity of background, experiences, culture, and ability all affect learning and each factor adds, when integrated into the learning environment, to total understanding.
   e. Creative problem solving and critical thinking skills can only be taught in a learning atmosphere that allows for student to student interaction which encourages expression of how individuals problem solve and engage in critical thinking.
   f. Relevance regarding learning is self-perceived and is built around choice and determined by degree of indepth involvement.

3. The change from student work being evaluated by a teacher inspectorship model to one of student self-assessment.
    a. One of the important lifelong skills is knowing how to do self-evaluation.
    b. Self-evaluation is dependent upon interest, pre-set goals or aims, a set plan of action, and energy employed to meet the goals or aims.
    c. The skills and choice to do self-evaluation will lead to pride in work and the completion of high quality products.
    d. In order to become skilled at doing self-evaluation, the individual student must be taught the specific skills necessary and have ample experiences to perfect the skills.
4. The present classroom management of behavior and work product being primarily managed by fear and/or punishment will change to a management style that is noncoercive and is built around a communication model that fosters negotiation and compromise.
    a. Fear, either by reward or punishment, is detrimental to quality work and needs to be removed as a classroom management procedure.
    b. When a system of communication that teaches respect, negotiation, and compromise is used as the basic classroom communication style, a life-long positive communication process is developed.
    c. Quality work is an inherent aspect of all people and classroom management that has involvement, respect, and encouragement fosters the trait.
5. Quality student learning requires time to become flexible to ensure student in-depth exploration of subject matter and classroom teachers creativity be utilized for planning meaningful lessons.
    a. Quality work, quality products, and pride in work result from in-depth exploration of subject matter.
    b. To be able to understand the complexity of information and apply it for positive results all subject matter areas must be interrelated.
    c. In-depth exploration of learning requires the classroom to be structured in a manner that allows the teacher to have maximum control over time to ensure non-fragmentation of learning.
    d. When options of time for class periods, school day, school year, and continuous years of teaching of same teacher/student exist, learner needs and teacher needs will be better met, resulting in quality learning and quality teaching.
    e. Multi-aged grouping in the same classroom provides a rich learning environment by having age-driven levels of achievement, positive peer role models, acceptance of individual differences, and multiple options for classroom management.

6. A program of continuous in-depth parent-teacher "partnershiping."
   a. Parent-teacher-student partnership is long term and has in-depthness as its goal.
   b. Teacher, parent and student form a continuous communication network, planning and sharing the responsibilities that lead to effective classroom learning, quality parenting and quality student learning.
   c. The responsibility of an administrative guidance team, classroom teacher and the individual student be defined in a way that will ensure the parent as a partner in the education process of the student.
   d. The parent will be empowered to use the school as a resource, as a base for learning, sharing and continuous development of more effective parenting skills.

As the classroom teachers master the management skills, the classroom will evolve to one that emphasizes individual student and group collaborative driven learning, the acceptance and encouragement of individual differences, indepth quality student developed learning products, the encouragement and reinforcement for quality work, students' abilities to set individual or group self-learning goals, accomplish self-evaluation of their work and products. The teacher will understand and have the skills to assess student learning styles and build learning experiences around student interest and talents. The classroom then becomes the environment that is receptive to meet the diverse needs of all students and quality learning is the outcome.

The two individuals that have been the major influence on my quest to understand quality and its need to be the basis for teaching and learning are Dr. William Glasser and Dr. W. Edwards Deming.

Dr. William Glasser is the single greatest influence on my teaching career. I became interested in his ideas pertaining to the how and why people behave as they do and his ideas on what schools should be like after listening to him speak in the late 1960s. I followed up by attending workshops sponsored by The Educator Training Center and became certified as a person skilled in the use of Reality Therapy. My association has continued over the past twenty-two years and was further solidified eight years ago when I was able to develop and implement a concentration of study based upon Control Theory and Reality Therapy as part of the University of Wisconsin—La Crosse Master's Degree in Education and Professional Development.

The six principles that I believe constitute the basis for quality classroom management are all based upon the understanding of Control Theory. A prerequisite to the reading of this book is to read the following books: *Control Theory in the Classroom*, and *The Quality School*, both written by Dr. Glasser and published by Harper Row Publishing Company.

Dr. Hal Hiebert, a friend and colleague of mine, introduced me to the ideas of Dr. W. Edwards Deming, and I immediately saw connections with Dr. Glasser's ideas about Control Theory and Dr. Deming's work regarding quality management. The next time I heard Dr. Glasser speak, I was elated and excited to hear him talk about Dr. Deming and to hear him use quality management ideas as they relate to what constitutes effective teaching and managing.

I then became a reader and student attempting to understand Dr. Deming's fourteen management principles, as well as to continue to learn from Dr. Glasser as he expanded and incorporated Dr. Deming's principles into the quality school movement. It is the influence of these two philosophies that has inspired me to develop the ideas around the six principles of quality classroom management.

This book is based upon my interpolation of the fourteen Deming management principles and how they pertain to classroom management. The book is not about total quality management, which is a systems approach to management. I believe total quality management principles need to be incorporated into total school system management, and that school administrators be trained to use total quality management to create systemic change that reinforces quality classroom management. This book is not attempting to interpret or apply total quality management principles to enhance systemic change, but is designed for classroom teachers.

The six management points are to assist the classroom teachers to expand their management repertoire, in the process of teaching and learning, the two primary players are the teachers and the students. All systems in the school district must be designed to support this relationship. This implies that the two primary decision making groups are the teachers and the students, and they must become empowered to direct teaching and learning. Administrators must learn how to serve the teachers, who are the first line management, and teachers must learn how to serve the students, who are the workers.

2

The Starting Point: Understanding Quality

As I became familiar with Dr. Deming's philosophy and his techniques to incorporate quality into the industrial complex, I realized that I had spent minimal time contemplating quality on either a personal or professional level. I experienced my personal and professional worlds, liked what I did in both, received personal fulfillment, but seldom reflected on particular experiences as quality equated. I became more aware of my personal non-judging attitude, and realized that I was missing out on an opportunity to enrich my life by not having decided upon quality qualifiers.

I then started to ask other adults if they had developed quality qualifiers in their personal and professional world, and found out I was like the majority. As I discussed quality with them, I asked if they could identify an experience or a product they had completed that they would judge as quality, and all could. They then would proceed to explain what the elements were that caused it to have a quality rating. As I listened, there emerged central themes and perceptions that I now believe are basic when understanding quality.

During the many personal discussions, the following six quality qualifiers became apparent. Some, or all, of them were incorporated into each of the individuals' personal evaluation of quality.

1. Quality is based upon continuous improvement.
2. Quality is commitment to hard work.
3. Quality is an internally developed, continually changing personal definition.
4. Quality is derived from self-imposed standards.
5. Quality is formed through relationships.
6. Quality is connected to uniqueness.

I believe the qualifiers are basic when understanding quality and developing a quality managed classroom.

Quality is based upon continuous improvement. Historically, quality as a concept has not been an integral part of classroom teachers' vocabulary or thinking. When I ask teachers about quality and how it impacts their teaching, the most common response is: "We haven't really thought about it." As we continued to discuss quality, the most common conclusion that is reached is that quality is a by-product of what transpires when students do good work. The teachers relate that the word is seldom used as feedback to students or as a criteria for assessing student work. Yet, I find that the first major hurdle to get over when discussing quality classroom management with teachers is the perception that I assume they are not quality teachers. They become quite indignant, defensive, and challenging. I know the word fuels an emotion in them by their reactions. We have to get past this point of assuming that what is presently done is not quality, and that every aspect of the teaching process will need to be discarded and re-invented to ensure quality.

Quality is a process of evaluation that is driven by the realization that continuous improvement is the basic element. No one ever reaches the final degree of perfection. Whatever technique, strategy, or materials that are being employed can be improved, and as they are improved the quality increases.

Continuous improvement is a difficult concept for classroom teachers to operationalize. They work in an environment that is top-down managed and dictated by absolutes, the contract work day is 8 to 4, students will demonstrate specific test scores, specific curriculum material will be covered, classroom discipline will meet certain specific expectations, class size will be x number of students, and the system becomes overwhelming, and survival instead of continuous improvement becomes the standard. I understand why there is frustration when the word quality is applied to classroom teaching. Teachers are doing the best they can to survive, and the initial challenge of quality becomes the straw that breaks the teachers' level of acceptance.

The first step of moving to a quality managed classroom and develop quality learners is to realize and accept the fact that whatever is presently being done can be improved. What is presently being done is quality because it is the best that you know how to do, but it is always in the process of changing, and can become higher quality.

Quality is commitment to hard work. The fact that students have not connected quality to classroom learning becomes obvious when it is discussed with them. I have personally interviewed two hundred students, fourth grade through high school, pertaining to quality. All two hundred find it difficult to define the word, yet all can find examples of what they believe emulates quality. The younger students most often give examples of quality that represent material objects, such as toys, athletic equipment, clothes, etc. The examples change in middle school and focus on competition, sports, entertainment, and often name personalities in the entertainment and sports professions. Music groups and specific selections of music are commonplace responses, as well as clothing. High schoolers report quality in extra curricular events, music, clothes, and specific people they know, often citing their friends, parents, and teachers.

Only ten of the two hundred cited academic learning as an example of quality. Herein lies a significant connection to one of the causes of the breakdown regarding student motivation. What motivates students to work hard is that the outcome will be quality which causes the student to sense pride and accomplishment and provides them with the incentive to continue to work hard. Quality demands commitment, hard work, in-depth exploration ending in the creation of a product that has pride as its outcome. The student will never connect classroom learning and quality until the standards of work and product completion are based upon high standards.

This missing connecting link of quality to academic learning is the fact that students can get by with doing minimal, low quality work. They sense minimal pride upon completion of a product. One of the high schools where I am working with teachers to develop quality classrooms has asked that I talk with the students and get a student perspective of what will increase quality in the classroom. One of the common responses I hear is that the classroom is boring and offers no challenge. Boring and no challenge are synonymous, and what the students want is to need to work hard so there is pride in what they have accomplished.

To inspire students to do quality work, it must become the basic process which permeates all work. Quality is not a single aspect of a lesson plan, but is the end product of that lesson plan. Quality incorporates a personal level of commitment, a challenge, and hard work to produce a product which will add immediate or long-term meaning to their individual lives. Integrating this into the classroom can be done only when it is a continuous, ongoing experience.

Quality is an internally developed, continually changing personal definition. I had the opportunity to work with a class of eight-year-olds in an exercise designed to begin defining quality. I asked each student to first produce his/her idea about what quality was and depict the idea in written or picture form. They then were to discuss the idea with a small group of peers and then connect their individual products to form a mural. The artistic result was impressive. However, when discussing their ideas of quality, the students didn't want to focus on their own work. Instead, they attempted to get me to tell them which individual art piece was "the best." It became clear that the individual student's concept of quality was centered around competition and outside evaluation. They wanted me, as the teacher, to choose the one piece of work that depicted "the best," which they then could use as the criteria for quality.

This experience shouldn't have surprised me. When one thinks about the world that eight-year-olds live in and the connections they have to quality, why wouldn't they equate it with competition and external evaluation? Product advertisement cleverly associates quality as the "best one," the entertainment industry with its awards for "best one," the educational world and its attempts to find the "best one,"—the list goes on. Students presently exist in a world that imposes a concept of "best one" to quality. Until they have the opportunity to explore it in their classrooms, they will be manipulated by an imposed definition that is external and used as a means to influence their behavior for specific gains.

The reason students cannot define quality, but can give examples, is clear: it is viewed by them as external. Quality is used to sell or promote and is perceived as something provided for them. They don't connect the concept of quality to themselves or to what they do, so there is no connection of quality and the academic work they produce.

The realization that quality is an individual definition, influenced by present knowledge and values, and is in continuous redefinition is difficult to teach. As teachers, we have to alter our present understanding and behavioral responses to assist students to develop self definitions of quality that can be used for self-evaluation, they will reach a point where the evaluation of any given situation will not need outside validation. When the need for external validation no longer exists, quality will prevail.

Quality is derived from self-imposed standards. The evaluating of quality has two points of reference: the product and the process used to develop the product. The traditional, individualized classroom has predominantly used products for the definition of quality. The emphasis has been on individual students' produced work such as writing examples, math computation sheets, oral reading, answers to reading comprehension questions, completed assignments, and test scores. The completed work is then evaluated by the teacher, and the degree of quality is determined by the standards of the teachers. Different teachers have different standards, and students learn to set their standards based upon what they believe the teacher wants.

The process removes the students from having the opportunity to learn how to set their own standards, and teaches them to rely upon an external definition of quality. Twenty percent of the students choose to continue to work for the external validation and become what is defined as the successful student. The other eighty percent, due to minimal success, do just enough to get by, or eventually develop behaviors that reject the system and become the problem students that are the discipline problems and or low achievers. Low quality work for this eighty percent becomes the standard.

For high standard work to become the norm for the majority of students, the system has to be changed. Instead of using the outside expert standard setter concept of high quality, the individual student must become empowered and taught the process of self-imposed standards. This change requires a belief system that students want to be successful workers, will have pride in their work, will work hard to achieve their wanted outcomes, and will continue to set higher quality standards for themselves.

The teachers' role in assisting students to develop high standards is to have set personal high standards for their own classroom performances and to continually project belief systems that indicate that each student is capable of high standard work. The student, having the confidence of the teacher, then develops a belief system in themselves that equates into high production and quality outcomes. The factor that makes the difference is the continual feedback of the capability of doing quality work, not praising of the completed work.

Quality is formed through relationships. Education, in its attempt to document academic achievement, has narrowed the thinking and research on educational outcomes to be specifically subject matter defined, consisting of isolated facts or applying isolated skills in reading and mathematics, and paper and pencil tested. The success of the learner is primarily documented by his/her ability to recall isolated facts or apply specific isolated skills during group testing sessions, and has placed minimal importance based upon their ability to relate. The data is then predominantly derived from classrooms that are managed on an individualist learning format and reflect isolated student learning.

The development of cooperative learning by Drs. David and Roger Johnson, University of Minnesota, was a significant break from the traditional individualized teaching model and challenged the idea that students learn best in individualized managed classrooms. Their work, with a strong research base, has proven that learning through relating is as or more effective than individualized learning, with added positive outcomes of increased motivation, development of social skills, appreciation of individual differences and an attitude that school and learning are fun. What they have documented is relative learning is more quality than individualized learning.

The more I understand quality, the more I realize that relationships are what drive quality. Student developed products that reflect quality are to a great extent produced by the teacher's ability to positively affect the attitude of the student through empowerment of the individual and creating a positive team relationship. The attitude of the worker and how they relate to fellow workers are as important as the skills needed to produce the actual product.

I am presently involved in a school where a change in principals has changed the quality of the teaching. The teachers had been working in an environment where the principal had skillful relationship management techniques. She was continually empowering the staff decision making power, assisting them to develop the necessary decision making skills, encouraging them by personal conferences that related to their teaching skills, continually sharing interest in their personal lives, and expounding a belief in their worth and expertise. She chose to relocate, and was replaced by a principal who was detail oriented, needed a high degree of control, wanted all decisions to be focused through him, and seldom related to the teachers, either on a professional or personal level. After three years of working under the new principal, the atmosphere of the school has completely changed. No one visits the teachers' lounge, teachers arrive at the moment the master contract states, and leave at the end of the day according to the contract, seldom is there shared success, absenteeism demonstrated by used sick leave days increased, and when I am in the building I sense an atmosphere of apathy. The enthusiasm is gone.

Classroom management operates the same as effective principal management, quality is based on the management of the relationships.

Quality is connected to uniqueness. It is very difficult for a school staff and the individual teacher to take the leap of faith to commit to continuous improvement that drives quality. Teachers have a high level need for security, and by everyone being the same, the need is fulfilled. Schools follow the same pattern; being the same is viewed as the right way. School choice has as one of its promotional components, the idea that a student will have a greater opportunity for success because they will experience school in a different, more unique way. Some have a specific subject matter emphasis, example being the magnet schools with an art-drama, math-science, truck driving, etc., emphasis. Some schools promote continuous learning based upon each student's ability to progress due to individual development instead of chronological age. Some promote a program that emphasizes a close student teacher relationship due to small class size. Each school promotes its uniqueness that makes it a special place for students.

When I work with a school staff that is making the decision to move toward a quality school, there is always the wanting of the blueprint for quality. A major setback comes when they find out there isn't one—only ideas that will help each staff member to modify and adapt their individual teaching style to become continuously improved, which causes the school to change and define their uniqueness. As there is continued improvement, there is continued change, and the result is a sense of pride, ownership, and being special and positively different, unique.

THE EXTRA-CURRICULAR MODEL
FOR QUALITY CLASSROOM MANAGEMENT

The persons best able to define a quality classroom are the workers that produce the learning products—the students. As I mentioned earlier, they seldom associate quality with academic learning, but starting in middle school and throughout high school, they do relate quality to the extra curricular programs they participate in. Drama, forensics, orchestra, band, and the numerous athletic programs are quality. As classroom teachers, we need to know the variables that cause the student to associate the various activities as quality, and then begin to modify and integrate the variables into classroom management.

The following chapters of this book focus on discussing and proposing ideas that will assist in the movement of classroom management to continuous improvement based upon six management principles, definitions of quality,connectiveness,'inspectorshipping" to self-assessment, noncoercion, time, and its relationship to quality and long term in-depth relationship with parent, and incorporate the students' extra curricular perception of quality. I have had numerous teacher groups analyze extra curricular activities regarding quality. There is a consensus that the following fifteen points provide the students with a perception of what constitutes quality in school. Each point is followed by a statement that I believe validates the reason it constitutes quality.

1. Recognition. What drives the individual participant to work hard and achieve success is the dual recognition of peers and an outside audience. They work hard because they believe they have the possibility to be a star and in doing so, will have recognition and a place of importance honored them. The chance of participating in the big play that wins the game, the outstanding performance that carries the play, the solo in the band concert or chorus performance that brings the audience to its feet, the article or picture in the local newspaper, etc., all lead to recognition and a self perception of quality.

2. Time. The coaches are not tied to the stringent time restraints of classroom teaching. When you need the additional time to reach perfection, you can take it. If it takes an extra half hour, a special practice session, or sometimes just an extra ten minutes, it is okay.

3. Choice. The participant makes the choice to become part of the team, and the choice indicates his/her ownership into the team's successes and failures. The fact that they can choose to quit, as well as continue, places the responsibility of participation and perfection totally upon their own sense of personal commitment.

4. Talent. They join the activity because they believe they will become skilled in an area where they have talent. The first step in the process of becoming good at anything is having the attitude that I am capable, then hard work that leads to perfection is reasonable. The opportunity for continued self and coach evaluation of their talent continues and verifies their belief in themselves. Those who choose to stay with the activity continue to believe in their talents and perceive value in the hard work that leads to perfection.

The classroom, instead of focusing on talents, becomes a place that often places emphasis on deficits, with remediation becoming the norm. Extra time and energy are employed to remediate the deficit areas, with additional homework. They have no choice but to continue, and the de-emphasis of talent projected by deficit remediation causes them to perceive the classroom as a non-quality experience. As quality classroom managers, we must perceive ourselves as talent developers and emphasize learners' strengths over their weaknesses.

5. Belonging. Participation in extra curricular activities opens the pathway for in-depth meaningful relationships. One of the starting points for meaningful relationships is built around the point of finding others with like interests. The chosen activity automatically fulfills the want.

6. Interdependence. The fact that the team achieves success as each individual improves creates a reciprocal positive drive for perfection. The fact is compounded as the team continues to sense improvement, the stronger the need to individually improve. The successful coach understands the need to create this relationship amongst the players, and the super star teams are de-emphasized. Instead, each player becomes an integral part of the team, and success is built around interdependency.

7. Organization. The coach is continually working with individuals or in small groups, perfecting a skill or skills, that eventually come together in the total performance. The team members accept the coach's organizational style as they realize the rewards of peer improvement in the team efforts. The effect of having to continually demonstrate the skill, receive continuous feedback, and have opportunity to improve is not perceived as hard work, just how a coach coaches.

8. Success is easy to measure. The outcomes are performance based, and the process for continual improvement is highly defined. The coach is personally involved during the process and becomes an integral part of the improvement process by demonstration and feedback. With continuous improvement, the final product can become a win, an enthralled audience, or a superior score.

9. Competition. There is continual need for self improvement as the possibility exists of some one else taking your position. The chairs in the orchestra, the starting positions, and the lead in the play all depend on the need to improve.

10. The need to emulate our heroes. In all the performance arenas there are the nationally recognized stars. They are highly publicized, highly paid, have a large, dedicated audience, and provide a model.

11. Multi-aged. The performance groups all are multi-aged, building into the group the opportunity for older, more accomplished students to have the respect of the younger students. They become integral models and continue to work hard to keep their respect and set the future for the team. The younger students work hard to become like the models, oftentimes having the older models assist them in the process.

12. Develops leadership, admiration, and cooperation. The respect for skill attainment becomes the norm, the student that excels becomes the respected leader. The higher the skill level, the greater the probability of team success, and cooperation becomes a positive force.

The classroom often works in the opposite way. The student that can and does excel academically is rejected by the majority as they believe his/her accomplishments will either reflect their accomplishments, or cause them to have to work hard to reach their level of accomplishment. They see the excelling student working hard and assume that they will be expected to do the same, consequently it is easier to bring the student down to their level than to work hard and improve. The students that have developed the skills of equalization become the respected and alienation of the gifted becomes the norm.

13. The coach believes his/her team members are capable of high performance. Due to a process of selection and continual performance assessment, the student is encouraged to continually improve. The coach is projecting a belief that you are capable, have perfected degrees of the skills necessary, and can always become better. It is this belief in the student that provides them with the strength to excel.

14. Mentorship relationship. The coach has proven him/herself as accomplished by being or having been a performer. The player knows this and respects the coach and wants to perfect the same skills. The perception is that the coach has something the player wants. The coach has selected the player by making a judgment that he/she is capable of becoming a skilled competitor. The learner relationship can now become intact. Coach, you have skills that I want to develop; player, you have the ability to develop the skill.

15. The activity is perceived as fun. Even though the outcomes require discipline and hard work, the student perceives it as fun.

Each of the fifteen factors have equal importance. As the student individually works toward perfection, the process of reaching perfection is highly structured and provides continual feedback. There is a defined, performance-based final outcome and a personal sense of accomplishment as the student proceeds toward quality.

The challenge of quality classroom management is to develop and continually improve systems and techniques that encourage these fifteen principles.

Modeling of Quality

As students discuss and solidify their own definitions of quality, they need to become aware of significant others that exemplify quality. Significant others are peers, parents, teachers, athletes, academicians, entertainers, musicians, and artists. Art, music, and physical education teachers have a major role in assisting students to internalize quality by providing activities for quality participation as well as introducing individuals that have quality lifestyles, philosophies, and proven performance.

Peer modeling, regarding quality, is always present and represents optimal opportunity for development. The classroom atmosphere needs to be one where students feel comfortable and secure and are encouraged to share their quality ideas, definitions, and work products. The process of using peer quality modeling is based upon the fact that what the individual student defines as quality must be respected by everyone and is self-initiated. Ideas shared, work displayed, and definitions shared are all volunteered by the individual and should never be judged as quality by another peer or teacher. The student needs to explain their reasoning as to why something is quality and discussion might follow, but the discussion is never judgmental. Students' ideas or work are never chosen as the best in the class—instead, it always represents the individual's perception of quality.

When students are working toward quality academic products, they must have continual exposure to examples of quality work. The models need to be present when initial work begins, with additional models available as the product is developed to a quality level.

Models that are representative of individualistic work should be collected from former students' work or different classrooms and placed in a teacher portfolio. No student work from the present classroom should ever be held up as a model. The social implications that result from this process are counterproductive as the student, if he/she plays the role of model, stands a strong chance of being stereotyped as teacher's pet or "the brain" with peer disapproval as the outcome. On the other hand, they may deny the assigned role, oftentimes resulting in future low production work to avoid the role.

The classroom teacher is in a position of continually modeling quality. The role of modeling quality is often misunderstood and is perceived as inspecting students' work to ensure quality, which is the topic of Chapter 4: inspectorship and self-assessment.

The quality modeling that needs to be incorporated into classroom action is the sharing of what constitutes each teacher's personal quality world. Students want to know about their teachers' personal experiences and enjoy hearing about what their teachers do and how they feel as they experience everyday living. They need to hear their teachers share a quality book, a quality meal, a quality talk, a quality sunset, a quality movie, and so forth. As teachers share quality, they need to explain why the experience was quality, and encourage discussion that assists the students to apply quality understanding to their everyday experiences.

DEVELOPING THE CLASSROOM DEFINITION OF QUALITY, THE CLASSROOM QUALITY OPERATIONAL CHART

The student, in order to develop understandings of quality and apply quality as their determiners for self evaluation, must be able to continually discuss, analyze, share, and redefine its meaning. Quality is a continual discovery that changes with new knowledge and experiences. It is the dynamics of change that shape the definitions.

The classroom teacher needs to have a plan that allows for the definitions and redefinitions. The plan promotes the ideas of change and is forever evolving. It needs to be student driven and student determined. Do not make teacher-student derived lists of quality and post them. They have the connotation of being final as once the list is derived, the activity is done, and we move onto the next activity. The students say what they think the teacher wants to hear, and the entire process is teacher driven by editing.

In the elementary school, the creation of a Classroom Quality Operational Chart is effective. The chart needs to be large, posted in a conspicuous place, and have the possibility for recording a continual flow of ideas.

The process is started by the teacher using the word quality in his/her common responses to students. He/she relates the word to relationships, atmosphere, products, and aesthetic appreciations. When the word is used, there is no definition or qualifier given, as the use of the word is to cause the students to begin to question the meaning of its use. When the students bring to question what is meant by quality, the teacher notes the need to define the word by advocating that it should be discussed at an appropriate class discussion. The class then defines the meaning of the word and, if they choose to, places the definition into the Classroom Quality Operational Chart. The chart has four columns: atmosphere, relationships, products, and aesthetic appreciation. The class decides where the definitions need to be placed, how it is to be stated, and then selects a class member to do the recording. In the lower primary grades, the teacher aids in the recording.

The chart is continually expanded throughout the school year. As the students become familiar with quality they will also begin to use it to describe what they are doing, feeling, and seeing and their use of the word should be viewed as a possible indicator for a class definition. Entries on the chart are always student discussed, student defined, and student chosen for recording.

John Koehn, a friend and associate of mine, suggests that once the students have definitions in the different columns of the chart, they be given the power to problem solve what needs to be done to have continual classroom quality. A buzzer or bells are placed in the room, and when an individual student perceives quality is being violated, he/she rings the bell, and all work and activity stops. The situation is then described, and small groups immediately problem solve, solutions are shared, definitions developed, and then work or activity resumes. I totally agree with the idea—as students become empowered to create quality, quality will prevail.

3

Connectiveness

Connectiveness refers to developing the classroom in a way that the learner feels secure which enables them to create quality work. This implies the need to break down barriers by removing fear, accommodating uniqueness, and eliminating the environment of surface relationships. In the process of developing connectiveness, three dynamic relationships emerge, all of which are necessary for quality work. Each will be discussed in this chapter. The first one will be connectiveness as it pertains to the classroom teacher and his/her ability to interact with students. The second aspect will address having the students connect with each other, thus developing close personal relationships with a sense of completeness and totalness as they interact with their learning peers in the classroom. The third aspect of connectiveness will address how we can make classroom learning relevant to each individual student on a personal basis.

TEACHER/STUDENT RELATIONSHIPS

Research consistently reports that if students are going to have positive learning experiences, they must sense that their teacher cares for them on a personal level. They must perceive themselves as worthwhile individuals. This fact is so consistent in journals and educational textbooks that it has become one of the most recognized aspects of creating an environment conducive for quality learning.

However, often this research information is misunderstood. Language such as the following—the teacher should be approachable; the teacher displays patience and empathy; the teacher is sensitive to preferred communication patterns of individuals and groups; the teacher avoids destructive criticism, embarrassing or demeaning comments, etc.—leads to the teacher misinterpreting his/her side of the relationship. Being approachable with patience and empathy, while paying attention to preferred communication patterns does not ensure a connective relationship. It insures an environment of overall stability that we find in impersonal settings such as a visit to the doctor or the driver licensing building. Common courtesy dictates approachability with preferred language usage, yet the classroom must move beyond this impersonal setting. We must replace the stereotypical statements about teacher-student relationships and focus on the need of relating. Students need to experience their teacher on a mutually personal level.

When I sit down with individual students and ask them what they need in order to know they have a quality teacher, their most reported response is that they need to feel their teacher respects them. If they have any perception that they are not respected by the teacher, they report a dislike for the class and have a tendency to reject all aspects of the school environment. When I hear students talk about respect from the teacher, it leads me to ask: "Just what is it about a teacher that causes you to know that you are respected?"

There is a common response to the question regardless of the grade level, maturity level, or academic level of the students. The response is, "A good teacher sees me as an important person, believes in me, and thinks I matter." They continually verbalize that the best teachers are the ones who "showed me that I am important by talking with and listening to me."

The perception of the students' sense of importance precedes their ability to create quality work. If we expect the student to be a quality worker and produce quality work, we must spend the time and energy to send the message that you are important and capable of producing quality work. We must recognize the importance and necessity of our students to have this perception of connectiveness as it becomes a major motivation for quality work.

Students begin the year wondering (and hoping) that the teacher will recognize them in a way that will allow them some freedom and control over their daily classroom life. They see connection in terms of what the teacher thinks of them and believes they have the ability to accomplish. This is a far cry from the approachable with sensitivity statements that educational research expounds.

Students connect with teachers who are willing to invest time, allow choice, and create trust as part of the connective relationship. To students, this runs at a much deeper emotional level than most teachers realize. It becomes apparent that each individual student perceives the teacher in their own special way, but what they're looking for is: "Will this teacher recognize me and when they do, will they recognize me in such a way that I can feel I'm an important person?"

In discussing student-teacher connection with teachers there is a slightly different perspective which emerges. Teachers, on the whole, do not perceive themselves as investors in meaningful relationships. Their message is: "The student who is motivated, involved, and producing work in my classroom is the one I have meaningfully connected with." As I continue to explore this idea, they relate that students who have a strong interest in the subject matter and who are willing to invest themselves in the work requirements are the ones who they get to know on a more personal level. These academic students are those who make up the twenty percent group—the ones who succeed at academic expectations. The teachers relate that it is the seeking out of information that leads them to meaningful connecting with students.

Academic success is a factor in a meaningful teacher to student connection. Students need to demonstrate interest and a desire for exploration into subject matter areas if they are to create quality work. However, teachers need to begin to perceive themselves as investors in their students' whole lives. This implies a daily relationship which moves beyond academic areas into personal and emotional involvement.

Teacher responses during parent-teacher conferences, particularly in the middle and high school, were frustrating as Carole and I sat down to discuss our children. The teacher would get out the grade book and want to talk to us about grades. This really was of very little interest to us. What we really wanted to know was what they are like in the classroom. Do they talk to the rest of the students? Are they part of the group? Do they positively respond to you when asked to do things? Are they inclusive of you and were they concerned about you as a teacher? Those were the kinds of issues we wanted to address at parent-teacher conferences.

As soon as we told the teacher that we weren't interested in grades and, in fact, we didn't care to look at the grade books, there was always a look at us as though we were strange. There was a pause as the teacher grappled in his/her mind to understand (or possibly accept) just what it was that we were asking. After it truly registered, the teacher would look at us with an expression of desperation. I sensed in that look that the teacher was actually saying, "I really don't know those things about your child." It was apparent that little personal connection had been reached between our daughters and their teachers. They were all successful according to the academic standard, yet we often felt that they seldom created quality work. Now that they are adults, they admit they often played the system to succeed on a standard of non-quality work.

It seems that in each classroom there are those few unique students who personally relate to the teacher as the teacher relates to them. When we reflect on a particular class and try to recall each student, there is always a significant number of them that aren't included in this "I know you as a person" relationship. We have made no connection, we know nothing about their lives, ideas and plans, and they, in turn, seldom saw the class as a place where positive learning experiences occurred.

The ultimate connection of student to teacher and teacher to student is realized through the emergence of a mentor/learner relationship. A quality managed classroom is attempting to continually evolve in this direction. The movement requires the emergence of two thought patterns. One, from the student's peception it is the realization that the teacher has knowledge, skills and behaviors that the student wants, which fuels the need for a personal relationship. The second, from the teacher's perception is that the student has interest, motivation, and talent to accomplish what he/she wants to learn. When these two perspectives coincide, the environment for a mentorship relationship is created.

The kindergarten and first grade teacher usually experiences the student perception of a mentorship relationship. The enthusiasm to learn, the sense of importance when learning has been accomplished, the wanting to share what is learned, the anticipating of what will be learned next, and wanting to work on a project or assignment are all indications of a mentorship relationship, and are an integral part of the students' attitudes as they enter school and progress into first grade.

How to continue this enthusiasm for a mentorship relationship as the students progress from elementary to middle to high school becomes the complex question.

Neither of these realizations are easy to accomplish as the student approaches middle school. The student is maturing psychologically as he/she begins to separate from the adult relationships in his or her life (parents, teachers) to child relationships within the peer group, causing classroom management and learning to be more difficult.

One of the means to accomplish this separation is by rejecting work that is expected. This results in the teachers feeling that what they are teaching is not valued by the students. The teacher responds to the rejection of the required work by believing the student is not interested in the subject matter and the mentorship bond is broken. Once the bond is broken the separation becomes greater and the work finished that is quality diminishes.

There are four basic factors which create the environment for the possibility of a mentorship relationship.

Empowerment

The first is for the teacher to communicate a desire to share the responsibility of learning and teaching with the student. This implies that the student has the right to make major decisions about her/his own learning and the teacher believes she/he has the ability and desire to be successful. Dr. Deming states that the only time we will produce quality work is when the workers are empowered to make major decisions regarding the standards of the product and the manager believes in their ability to create a successful product.

The belief that a student wants to learn, has the ability to do quality work, needs to be provided structures and freedom to proceed, and will be able to select and produce a product to prove their interest and talent, are all perceptions that must be internalized for quality teaching.

These are not the beliefs that have been promoted in our present individualized classrooms. We have operated from a perspective of telling students what they should do, providing the materials to them to do what we have told them to do, the proliferation of workbooks, ditto sheets, and answer sheets, using reward/fear management to see that the work is done, and then evaluating them. The system of "do what I tell you to do" destroys empowerment and destroys quality work.

Enthusiasm

A second factor that promotes a mentor relationship is evident when the student, eager to learn, meets the teacher, eager to teach. This enthusiastic reciprocal relationship builds the mentorship. High energy learning is contagious.

Students quickly sense the enthusiastic level of the teacher and respond appropriately. We all have participated in classes where the energy has been high, time went fast, response levels were quick, learning was in-depth and meaningful, everyone sensed involvement and what was being taught became relevant.

An enthusiastic teacher is often the key to relevancy. Teachers commonly believe that relevancy of subject matter pertains to a student's seeing the subject matter as having a practical application to immediate or long term needs. Few students think in these concrete terms. A stronger factor for relevancy is the teacher's enthusiasm for teaching.

Self Disclosure

The third factor that evolves into a student wanting a mentor relationship is the ability of the teacher to be personable. Teachers must know how and when to self disclose. Some teachers appear to have a built-in capacity for knowing when to talk personally to the class and when not to. All of us have sat through classes where at the end of the semester or school year we know nothing more about the teacher than when we started. Much of the time the class was an ordeal, as it involved little or no personal interaction with the teacher.

We came in, sat down, listened (or tried to), and left to return the next day to the same situation. We often had a quiz or test on Friday and wondered, "Does this person have a personality, a life outside of school, a family; does he/she ever have fun?"

When discussing with students the ideas of "the quality teacher," they normally include in the conversation that such a teacher is a "real person." When I explore the "real person" phenomena and ask what it is, they explain that it's someone who is willing to share with them. I ask, "What does the teacher share?" They respond, "Well, they share with us about their family, about the kinds of things they like to do, sometimes they tell us about things they see, like plays or weekend trips; sometimes they tell us funny little stories about things that happened to them when they were our age." We connect with students when we relate to them on a personal level.

Respect of the Individual

The fourth factor of a mentor relationship is centered on the teacher's willingness to know each student as an individual. In most classrooms there are a few unique students who the teacher gravitates to and they return the favor, thus, a relationship develops. This reciprocal relationship is present for most of the twenty percent of those students who are successful. These so called good students that the teachers identify with on a personal basis are usually good in all their classes, involved in many aspects of school, and are positively known by all the teachers.

The "bad student" is also known by all the teachers, but seldom has an indepth relationship with any of them, and constitutes about twenty percent of the school population. The other sixty percent are the ones who come to class daily, do the work, don't excel but don't get in trouble and leave with little known about them.

When we talk about the world of connecting, the world of creating relationships with our students, the issue is not so much "empathy, displaying interest, and avoiding demeaning comments" as it is knowing the students on a personal level. When we present ourselves as reciprocal partners to the students and learn to disclose personal aspects of ourselves, then empathy, interest, and respect follow. As we develop a personal type of relationship with all our students and they in turn become confident to share aspects of their personal world, connectiveness evolves and the fourth foundation for quality is built.

CONNECTIVENESS STUDENT TO STUDENT

Just as teachers need to become involved with students on a daily personal level, so do students need to find connectiveness with each other. This is the second factor of connectiveness which must be addressed. The classroom must be a place of security and safety and this cannot happen without opportunities for students to develop an appreciation and understanding of each other. As the students personalize themselves with each other, the entire class builds an atmosphere of cohesiveness.

This cohesive variable requires the connectiveness, or bonding, of the individual students to each other and results in the class becoming a unified group. The focus is to create appreciation of each others' strengths and uniqueness, which enhances the realization that when students work together and have fun together, everyone profits. There are some specific grouping patterns that will promote cohesive management and will be explained in the last section of this chapter.

One of the most difficult aspects of connective management is to bring the classroom to the point where this sense of oneness or togetherness is present. There must be considerable time, effort, and management skill perfected to provide the structure and experience to have students relate to each other on both a personal and academic level. The outcome of student connectiveness happens when each individual student realizes the power that comes from unity.

As teachers are prepared for their teaching careers there is minimal time spent assisting them with the understanding of class cohesiveness. The traditional individualized classroom dominates their professional training and focuses on management styles that are behavior modification managed and emphasized individualized learner outcomes. Education began to realize the importance of class cohesiveness when the need for cooperative learning became apparent. As cooperative learning management skills developed, the understanding of how class cohesiveness affected positive learning became obvious.

With a limited exposure to the need and the opportunity to develop management skills for creating student connectiveness, it is no wonder that teachers who sense the need and have the desire to create cohesiveness feel inept with implementation.

Individualized classrooms have as their emphasis, subject matter learning, and academic outcomes become paramount. Elementary schools immediately assess student learning levels and quickly follow up with subject matter learning. The first day in the secondary school each class outlines the semester by handing out a syllabus, followed by a detailed explanation of the work involved and checking to make sure everyone has a textbook and an assignment notebook.

The quality managed classroom is different as time is spent working with the dynamics of the group by having them learn about each other, teaching them how to respond to each other, and building the idea of respect for individuals. Interpersonal group dynamics must be established at the beginning of the year and strengthened continually throughout the rest of the year. This connective environment must be created! It doesn't just happen.

Cooperative learning, as it is initiated, takes time due to the need to teach the social skills and provide the structure for the skills to be demonstrated. The job of teaching and monitoring the social skills is energy and time consuming. One of the concerns that emerges is: "Will all the subject matter be covered?" Teachers who perfect the management skills for cooperative learning and continue to use it as the school year progresses report that the class productivity increases, as does the quality of the work, and the subject matter is covered.

Taking time to create student connectiveness is time well spent and the outcomes attest to the fact.

Productivity and Cohesiveness

These two variables need constant balancing to ensure that quality work is produced and quality relationships emerge. Productivity refers to the creation of products that represent learning outcomes, and cohesiveness relates to the bonding of class members into a total unit.

If either of the two variables becomes over or under managed, the group will be unable to sustain effective working conditions, and quality work and quality relationships cease to exist. Productivity and cohesiveness are interdependent. The class designed to include both has whole class activities that, when completed, produce a positive accomplishment for every member. As individual members achieve and everyone profits, there is incentive to honor and assist each other and cohesiveness is now in place.

I have been asked, on occasion, to help teachers who had lost control of the class that they were teaching. After meeting with the teacher and observing the classroom, it always becomes apparent that one of the two variables was over emphasized and the other not understood. In most instances, productivity was the variable that was over emphasized and cohesiveness least understood. Total disaster results when neither are understood.

The first time, as a school principal, that I had to formally dismiss a teacher during the school year resulted from his inability to create any productive-cohesive balance. It occurred in a middle school general music classroom and the teacher's first concern was to produce productivity through the formal teaching of music principles, such as notes, scales, key signatures, and the like. This was met with less than general acceptance by the class and their non-acceptance was demonstrated by minimal productivity. The teacher then over compensated and totally withdrew production as an outcome, focusing totally on cohesiveness with no intended purpose of specifically teaching music. The students then took control of the room and would not allow him any managerial power. There must be a balance between productivity and cohesiveness.

This importance of productivity and cohesiveness is emphasized by researchers David and Roger Johnson, as they developed their model for cooperative learning which is an excellent technique to increase the quality of productive work. The prime factor which causes this increase is the cohesive aspect of small groups; we are all in this together and we will all profit from the outcome of the products, we will sink or swim together. The use of cooperative learning is a must in the quality managed classroom as it automatically creates the balance needed between productivity and cohesiveness.

A prime factor which inhibits the teacher from building class cohesiveness is the lack of proper modeling. The majority of teachers are products of past learning experiences where the message was individualistic learning and discipline demanded "Settle down and get to work, or else!" This message was first stated in elementary school and then followed them through undergraduate pre-teacher education.

As I have related before, the primary grades, which are effective for most young learners, understand and manage a significant amount of class cohesiveness. The day normally begins with class sharing, quality circle, or class meetings, time is spent playing together on the playground, and getting to know each other is an integral part of the learning process. This emphasis for cohesiveness begins to taper off around third grade and continues to diminish as a student progresses through the school years.

The middle schools philosophically advocate programs that incorporate teachers' performance that builds around the student needs for relating to peer and teachers, but program analysis shows more schools emulate secondary school principles than elementary. The emphasis on subject matter, taught in separate classrooms with no connection to other subject areas, time slotted into forty-five to fifty-five minutes, students moving from classroom to classroom, teachers seeing one hundred twenty-five to one hundred fifty students per day, testing, and grading become more deliberate and discriminatory, and indifference by teachers to students increases. The secondary schools heighten the process and the indifference increases, then general studies in university undergraduate schools cap off the model.

Seldom is there a significant connection between students and professors at the pre-teacher level. The mark of a successful class as perceived by professors is how many tests need to be passed and how many papers need to be written and when and if the standards are met, the class is over and next semester another group comes through. Seldom are the names of the students seen as important to know and attendance is documented by the fact that someone is occupying the assigned seat. This air of indifference toward the student, the projecting of superiority, lack of recognition of individual differences and emphasis on subject matter project a model that too often is emulated as a model of effective teaching.

Teacher training then professes a philosophy of respecting and developing individual differences, cooperative learning, teachers individually relating to students, integrated studies and hands-on experiential learning yet teach in the same indifferent, separated, and de-humanizing way that the students have experienced for the past nine years. And some of us wonder why the system doesn't change!

It is not impossible to create the classroom in such a way that students feel a connection with each other and with the teacher. Most students have a great potential for building friendships quite easily and it is never long into the school year before groups of friendships emerge. Just as they have a great capability for ridiculing each other they also have great capacity for compassion, understanding, and tolerance. Students need proper modeling, discussions, and teacher expectations that focus on connectiveness. The message is, "In this room we are a unified group of people who can and will depend on each other."

CONNECTIVENESS TO RELEVANCY

Relevancy has minimal meaning in education until we understand quality. Presently, in academic areas it is tied to work completed and the grade assigned. Therefore, in the teacher's perspective, the grading system and the grade assigned determine relevancy.

Students relate to academic learning the same way. The most common response to "what did you learn" is to repeat the grade that was assigned to the topic or subject. If you are getting top grades, school is relevant, what you are learning is secondary.

We have traditionally developed the entire classroom management system around the concept of producing top performers that are designated by their grades. The use of reward or fear, recognition, retention, remediation all attest to the idea of producing students who get good grades. The system continues to work for the twenty percent of the students that are capable of top grades—the remaining eighty percent see little or no relevancy to academic classroom learning.

The sense of obligation to produce top academic performers in all subject areas has permeated all areas of educational thinking. We can accept the fact that not all students are going to be top athletic performers, top musicians, top drama performers, or top artists, yet we believe all students will be top readers, mathematicians, problem solvers, scientists, and social scientists. This belief is one of the problems that causes irrelevance in school. In the attempt to make all learners top academic performers in all areas we have created classroom environments that have an impossible mission. To compensate for the impossible we have brought the student that is capable of top academic performance down to mediocrity and invested the majority of human and financial resources into attempting to raise all students to be top academic performers in all subject areas. As we bring down the potential top performers to mediocrity, irrelevance of school is the outcome; as we attempt to take the student that is not capable of top performance and force him/her to be a top performer, frustration occurs and the result is irrelevancy. In both cases quality is non-existent.

Relevancy Is Talent Development

Relevancy is the result of students having the opportunity to develop talents to a point of perfection, which then becomes quality. The quality managed classroom centers on individual learners' strengths and builds from this perspective. The quality school invests in talents and promotes the realization that not everyone is going to be a top performer in all areas.

When I discuss relevancy with students, they equate it to things they are good at. Relevancy is in their immediate world, not tied to developing skills that will add to the possibility of better life-long living. The little person learns the names and sounds of the letters of the alphabet because, as he/she masters each letter and sound, he/she feels success and senses an accomplishment, which constitute relevancy. They aren't learning the letters and sounds to be a reader—that comes later.

Relevancy isn't being in first grade so they can prepare for second grade: first grade for the first grader is relevant. They don't think like adults, who are always preparing for the future. Students, all the way through secondary school prepare for now and find relevancy when what they are doing has immediate purpose and can be developed to the point of quality.

The most successful and relevant school managed programs center around extra curricular programs. One of the many successful programs is football. It is amazing to watch the energy, pain, endurance, and discipline that is required of each football player as they prepare, week after week, for the Friday night or Saturday afternoon game. By far, the majority of players realize they aren't going to be NFL players, they will not make football a life-long sport and it is not teaching them everyday living skills—yet, they continue to work and produce. To produce this amount of work it must have a high degree of relevance. Why?

I taught in a school system that had one of the most successful high school football programs in the state. The coach understood motivation and its relationship to relevance. I was told he met one-on-one with each of his players. In that meeting, if they would commit to becoming a team player, he would guarantee them that he would work with them until they learned the skill of their position to the point that, whoever they played against, they would be better than the opponent. Now there is purpose for the hard work, you will be good at what you are doing, we will work until it is at a quality level, it is specific to your position and it will make a difference at the end of the week. The quality classroom manager must understand this sequence as the successful football coach did.

The quality classroom manager manages from the perspective of the students' talents, not from the lack of talents and realizes that the perfection of the talents is what motivates. The classroom de-emphasizes remediation and focuses on development of student talents and accepts the fact that not all students will be able to perfect all skill related learning areas.

Relevancy Is Peer Interaction

Relevancy is dependent upon a perceived idea that what I am individually doing is important in the eyes of my peers.

I've seen individual students invest a great amount of energy in a product and perfect it to a level of quality because they believed it would be valued by their peers.

This is the moment when individual performance moves to the point of we instead of me and relevancy becomes real. Relevancy is always connected to relationships, and in the life span of school age learners, peers are one of the significant connections. The quality classroom manager understands this need to build the classroom environment into one that projects opportunity for continuous peer interaction.

The power and sense of accomplishment that results when an individual is involved in a winning team is astronomical. It prompts quality individual performance, which becomes total team effectiveness, which calls for greater individual performance and the two needs of individual and team success reinforce each other.

Relevancy Is Dependent Upon Recognition by an Audience

The football player doesn't perfect his skills to a quality perfection level just to please his coach. An actress doesn't perfect her role to quality perfection just to please the director, the sax player doesn't perfect his music to a quality level just to please the band leader—no, the real reason is to be recognized at the moment of performance. In all the performing arts, the individual works for the moment of the performance; this is what is relevant. Each of the individual students has a picture in his/her mind of what constitutes quality and will work hard to reach perfection for recognition at the performance. The football player believes he will be outstanding and be recognized; the actress will be so strong in her role that the play will be a total success, and recognition will follow; the solo will be appreciated and recognized by applause and, hopefully, a standing ovation. The recognition by an audience is what differentiates and results in extra curricular activities having relevancy to students. Many educators believe that extra curricular activities are more relevant because the student chooses the activity and that certainly is a factor, but not many would choose the discipline and hard work if there wasn't a performance and the possibility of recognition. The teacher, like the coach or director, gives continual feedback and recognition, but is perceived by students as part of the process of becoming and is part of the expected establishment that promotes learning and performance. They are supposed to give recognition, it's part of their job. Parents fall into this same category.

The traditional individualized, same age, nine months long classroom has failed to recognize the need for relevancy. It doesn't. It can't compete with extra curricular activities that are individually and group performance based, are multi-aged in competition, support and promote development of individual talent, and provide multiple outlets for recognition.

The quality classroom manager understands the need for relevancy to be part of daily classroom activities and factors into the learning environment the characteristic of extra curricular activities. Each chapter of this book builds support for and suggests ways to create individual and group based academic learning, multi-aged and continuous years of student teacher involved learning, capitalize on student talents, and provide meaningful in-class audiences to honor academic achievement.

GROUPING PATTERNS FOR OPTIMAL CONNECTIVENESS AND ACADEMIC OUTCOMES

Connectiveness is synonymous with relationships and the following four grouping arrangements allow for optimum connectiveness of teacher to student and student to student. The specific grouping arrangements have all been teacher proven in elementary through high school classrooms. The four patterns are class meetings, task groups, base groups, and special needs groups. Each group arrangement has specific purposes, bases for formation, and facilitating skills. The grouping arrangements provide the infrastructure for quality, student driven learning.

Class Meetings

Class meetings are the outcome of work done by Dr. William Glasser. He created the technique in his early work with schools and writes on the techniques in one of his first books relating to effective schools, *School Without Failure*. I have continued to perfect the technique as it is part of the skill training program leading to the completion of the Control Theory/ Reality Therapy concentration in the University of Wisconsin—La Crosse master's degree in Education and Professional Development.

The class meeting is the backbone for effectively utilizing the various grouping patterns and is in constant use in the quality managed classroom. It is used for three primary purposes: to promote individual thinking skills when it is facilitated with open-endedness; motivation that leads to task grouping; and group processing. The meeting always takes place in a circle arrangement and the systematic creation of the circle must be thoroughly taught. The students must have a plan presented to them for the quick, systematic moving of their desks into a circle. The movement pattern is determined by how the seats are arranged for the majority of the day and they are more than likely in small grouping patterns or in rows. Each student must know where and when his/her desk is to be moved to form the circle. There should be no turmoil or confusion during the process and, after practice, it should take less than a minute for formation. Structure and purpose permeate the meeting.

Once the students are in a circle, they will become involved in discussion that is facilitated by the teacher. The development of the skills to facilitate the meeting is basic to the success of the meeting. The class meeting is not an open discussion that is allowed to go wherever the ideas and thoughts of the students lead. Instead, it is highly structured, with specific purpose, and skillfully facilitated.

There is considerable confusion among teachers of what class meetings actually are. They have heard or read about them and support the concept, but have had little opportunity to discuss, understand, and perfect the skills to successfully plan and facilitate the meetings. There is a tendency for the meetings to be single topic designed, non- to minimally-structured, and without a specific purpose in the total learning cycle. Some teachers define class meetings as putting the students in a circle and have them engage in a free-for-all discussion, either having no designated leader or a student leader.

This isn't a class meeting—it's called a fiasco, and the outcome is confusion and non-productive learning. The meetings are always planned with specific purposes and are teacher facilitated.

The facilitating skills are built around the ability to lead the students through a sequence of questions that progress from definition to personalizing and depending upon purpose to challenge (Figure 1).

The meeting always begins with the review of basic ground rules. The ground rules are formed by the group in some of the initial meetings and are always referred to in follow up meetings. The rules create an environment that assures the student that the meeting is a safe place to express their ideas or challenge the idea of one of their classmates. Three or four rules meet this requirement and, in elementary schools, should be posted as a reference point.

Level: Elementary   Name:
Topic: Pets   Date:
Ground Rules: Stay seated, raise hand, one person talk at a time, listen respect-
           fully, no put downs
Objective:
Type: Open meeting
Define Questions:
   1. What is a pet?
   2. What are some things we should think about before getting a pet?
   3. What is a veterinarian and what do they do?
   4. What is the Humane Society?
   5. What types of names are given to pets?
   6. What pets can be our 4-H projects?
   7. What are some strange types of pets?
   8. What is a pet show or pet exhibit?
Personalize Questions:
   1. What kind of pets do you have?
   2. Where can you get a pet?
   3. What kind of things do you do for your pets?
   4. What kind of things do our pets do for us?
   5. Do any of your pets ever get into trouble?
   6. What do you think is the best part about having a pet?
   7. What is the hardest part about having a pet?
   8. Can you name any famous pets?
Challenge Questions:
   1. What do you think the world would be like without pets?
   2. If you could put together a perfect pet, what would it be like?
   3. If you were a pet, what would you be and why?

Level: Third grade   Name:
Topic: Books   Date:
Ground Rule: Raise hand before talking, respect and listen to what others
                have to say, no put downs
Objective: To expand the students' knowledge of books and to become aware
              of why we read
Type: Open-ended
Define Questions:
  1. What are books?
  2. Who are books for?
  3. Why do we have books?
  4. Who reads books?
  5. What kinds of books are there?
  6. Who writes books?
  7. How can you get a book that you would like?
  8. What are some ways to read a book?
  9. Where do people read books?
Personalize Questions:
  1. What kind of books do you like to read?
  2. What is a favorite book of yours and why is it your favorite?
  3. When do you enjoy reading?
  4. Where is your favorite spot to read?
  5. Why do you like to read?
  6. Why do you think that reading books is important?
  7. If you don't care to read, what could you do to enjoy it more?
  8. How does your family feel about books?
  9. Would you rather watch TV or read a good book? Tell why.
Challenge Questions:
  1. If you were going to write a book, what kind of book would you write?
  2. How would our lives be different without books?

Figure 1.   Class Meeting Format

The rules pertain to respectful listening, assurance that ideas and expressions will be respected, and that confidentiality will be assured.

Examples of rules that are commonly used are: (1) only one person talks at a time; (2) give total attention to the person who is speaking by showing eye contact and listening; (3) all ideas expressed are accepted; (4) no put-downs; (5) it is good to disagree, but we disagree with what is said, not the person who said it; (6) what we discuss in our circle can be shared with others, but we never share what an individual person said; (7) anyone has the right to pass if they are asked a specific question or for an idea.

Defining

Once the rules have been agreed upon, the teacher may want to start the meeting with a warm-up question. The question is one that is non-confrontive and helps to get the students into a responding mood. The questions are normally fun and move quickly around the circle. After the warm-up, the students are engaged in discussion that leads to agreement of definitions of terms. During this part of the meeting, there is considerable debate and sharing of understandings related to what the individual student believes to be true. The questions focus the discussion by having the students relate the topic to a self held factual base and often the questions ask the student to relate the basis of his/her ideas. (Figure 2 provides a list of topic ideas for class meetings.) As the students work through this part of the meeting and share in each others' understandings, the topic is narrowed to a point where agreement of a definition or definitions is reached. It is of absolute necessity to reach this understanding and get agreements of understanding. When this doesn't happen, students continue to discuss topics or ideas from their individually held perspectives and the result is limited learning, as each student attempts to reconfirm their original thinking. There then is no challenge to grow in ideas or understandings as there is no crisis to resolve.

The discussion must go beyond each individual student attempting to convince someone that his/her idea is the only idea or way to do something. This is normally the longest part of the meeting and requires the facilitator to skillfully challenge and draw the other class members into thinking, challenging, and confirming thoughts and ideas that are being expressed, and yet not discourage ideas or become dominant by offering the teachers ideas or solutions to the concerns. The teacher has to systematically teach his/her self not to become dominant and instead to keep asking the pertinent questions to allow students' thoughts to predominate. Seldom does the teacher tell or suggest solutions of what is correct—instead they always ask another question.

The purposes of the defining questions are:

1. To cause the students to reach a level of agreement about a topic that focuses the direction for the completion of the discussion
2. To allow for individual perceptions to be expressed, challenged, modified, or confirmed
3. To encourage students to base their ideas on facts
4. To assist students to experience negotiation and compromise as their personal definitions evolve into group definitions

Family
1. Getting along with brothers and sisters
2. Getting along with parents
3. Getting along with relatives
4. Sharing with other members
5. Borrowing and loaning
6. Jealousy
7. Privileges
8. Family rules and regulations
9. Allowances
10. Family responsibilities
11. Family confidences
12. Family social activities
13. Family heritage
14. Religion
15. Favoritism
16. Disputes
17. Rights
18. Child abuse and neglect
19. Foods and nutrition
20. Private time
21. Bedtime
22. Health problems
23. Social peer pressures
24. Child differences
25. Problems due to family size
26. Self-discipline
27. Death

School and Friends
1. Rules
2. Activities
3. Subject
4. Making friends
5. Qualities
6. Playing
7. Interactions
8. Togetherness
9. Love
10. Playground
11. What makes a good teacher
12. Environment
13. Happy school
14. Friends in trouble—loyalty
15. Parents
16. Types of schools
17. Groups of friends
18. Equality
19. Politeness
20. Principal
21. School boards
22. Staff
23. Cleanliness
24. What makes a good friend

Media
1. Areas of news—sports
2. Concerns about media
   a. Advertising
   b. Programming
   c. Pornography
   d. General news—how much to believe (11 people killed)
   e. What and how much shall I let my children watch
   f. TV as discipline?
   g. Do you read a newspaper?
   h. Violence
   i. Reading and radio—to stimulate imagination
   j. TV in school? How do children feel?
   k. Favorite programs
   l. Football cards
   m. Money spent on records
   n. Pressures applied through media—advertising—Movies?
   o. Magazines—what kind do you like?
   p. What about magazines in local stores—availability (Girlie)

Figure 2.   Topic Ideas for Class Meetings

5. To provide the opportunity to hear how peers think and what they base their idea upon
6. To narrow the topic to an understandable level and limit it from going off on tangents

The specific questions have a what and why emphasis and often give the facilitator an opportunity to engage in a short three or four question mini conference with an individual student. This short conference is spontaneous and when it happens, it allows for the individual student to orally think his or her way through a situation or work on an understanding and provides opportunity for the rest of the class to build their own thinking ability based upon what they are hearing.

It is always a good idea to have a student draw together the varied ideas for definition. It trains him/her to listen and to assimilate what has been heard into statements. As they orally develop the statements which become the agreed upon definitions, encourage other students to suggest ideas and support the student as he/she moves toward a finished statement.

Personalizing

The meeting then focuses on having the students personalize their experiences pertaining to the agreed upon definitions. The personalizing aspect brings an experience basis to the discussion and encourages the student to relate their real life experiences to the topic. The experience must be related to actual happenings—readings they have done that relate, movies or television shows they have seen, discussion they have experienced or heard, or an expression of thought or ideas that they personally had about the agreed upon definition.

This is the most enjoyable part of the meeting as students listen to members of the class share their experiences and they gain an expanded understanding of each other. One of the significant outcomes of class meetings is the total class bonding that it creates and the personalizing part is a prime contributor to this outcome.

Purposes of personalization:

1. Increases the involvement as personal experiences are encouraged
2. Adds relevancy to the meeting as the students apply personal experiences to the discussion
3. Provides an atmosphere for humor and or seriousness

The personalizing part of the meeting should be short and students need to realize that not all the experiences will be able to be heard, but as future meetings are held, everyone will eventually have the opportunity to be heard. The personalizing questions are focused around when, how, and what if, and are reflective in nature as the students volunteer to personalize and the questions are responding to their presentations.

The teaching of the sequence of definition to personalization is complicated due to the fact that people normally responded first by personalizing. This is particularly true for young children and it will require set guidelines, purposeful teaching, and modeling to change the sequence.

Challenge

The third aspect of the meetings is centered on creating a final challenge, and the purpose of the meeting dictates the delivery of the challenge. If the meeting is an open class meeting, it is to set the stage for continued individual thinking. If it is a motivational meeting, it creates the crisis that will prompt small task group action to engage in work that results in a product aimed at a solution. The challenge is to create just enough crisis to arouse the students to continue to think or become involved in the small group that is seeking solutions.

Challenging questions are what the entire meeting is centered around. Challenging questions create the definitions as well as the personalizing portion of the meeting and lead up to the final challenging question that ignites either individual extended thinking or the group action.

Purposes of challenging questions:

1. To cause individual thinking to become focused, more in-depth, reality and relationship based, factually grounded or well thought out, hypothetically based, and fluently expressed
2. To cause clarity of thought by introspection or peer contribution
3. To create an atmosphere where individual thought can be defined through positive group interaction and not become defensive when ideas and thoughts are being examined

The questions are developed around the need to examine assumptions, look for relationships, request clarification, transfer generalizations, and stimulate in-depth examination. They are worded in a context that requires thinking and answering that has to be stated and extended. There should never be one word answers to challenging questions. Models will be provided.

The final igniter challenge questions follow the personalization phase and brings the focus of the topic into the forefront. When the question is asked, it should emit the wanting to offer immediate answers, suggestions, or solutions, and timing to allow for individual involvement to generate ideas, yet keep the responses from coming forth is critical. When you sense that a significant part of the class is reaching a point of being ready to engage in discussion, you end the meeting and if it is an open meeting, challenge them for continued individual thinking, or if it is motivational, you organize the groups for investigations and solutions.

Types of Class Meetings

Open Meetings. One of the class meeting types is the open meeting, and its primary purpose is the expanding of individual thought. They are normally meetings that are formed around topics that are fun to discuss and add interest to being a member of the class. One of the factors to consider, relating to the success of the meeting, is how much did the students enjoy the discussion.

The meetings are topical, normally single sessions, and each meeting stands by itself. The purposes of the open class meeting are:

1. To provide an opportunity for success experiences for each student through participation by talking or listening
2. To promote a positive self-concept for each student: "What I have to say is acceptable and worthwhile."
3. To build involvement—a trusting, caring relationship between teacher and student, and among students
4. To provide opportunities for insightful, creative, critical, and divergent thinking
5. To furnish a channel for relevancy through discussion of subjects interesting and exciting to students
6. To build communication skills, listening, verbal fluency within the group, and language development
7. To learn the process of respectful interaction
8. To encourage responsibility within the group
9. To create and maintain an open, trusting atmosphere for learning

The two major responsibilities to prepare for an open class meeting are to pick a relevant topic and prepare questions. When a meeting fails to stimulate excitement and discussion, it normally is due to the fact that the topic had little relevancy to the students, not that the questions were inadequate. Franklin Elementary School in La Crosse, Wisconsin, has all the teachers trained to facilitate open class meetings and on the same day each week, each classroom conducts a meeting on the same topic. The guide questions are developed by teacher pairs and distributed a week in advance to allow for individual teacher preparation. Figure 3 provides a list of topics that have been used in kindergarten through fifth grade at the Franklin School.

The open meeting leaves the student with a challenge to think more about the topic. The meeting is concluded with this open ending. It is difficult for the teacher/facilitator to retrain his/her self to end the meeting with openness as it is in contradiction to the way teachers are trained. As teachers we were trained to end lessons with summation, to tell the students what was the important understanding from the lesson, to tell them what to remember, and let them know that they will be held accountable for knowing the specific information we highlight. The open meeting is built upon the concept that the student is capable of determining what is important, will sift out the significant meanings, and, due to his or her own need to understand, will continue to think about the meeting and the challenge (see Figure 4).

Motivational Class Meetings. A second type of the class meeting is to use it as a tool when teaching subject matter material, and it changes in purpose from being an open class meeting to one that has as its final challenge, motivation to do investigative individual or small group work. It is designed to create relevancy as the meeting engages the students in discussion that leads to the need to solve a problem. The students are taught that the motivational meeting always leads to individual or small group follow-up work and that they will be required to produce an outcome product that reflects their investigative work and knowledge base regarding the challenge.

The motivational meeting uses the same questioning sequence as the open meeting: define, personalize, and challenge. The definitive, personalizing, and challenging questions are developed around a topic that is an integral part of a given course of study. The teacher/facilitator leads the discussion to the point of challenge where the students are literally sitting on the edge of their seats wanting to begin to solve the problem. At this point the meeting immediately ends and the focus is directed to investigative work. Depending upon the nature of the investigation, the teacher has predetermined and planned the lesson to be individual, basic task group, or cooperative task group follow-up.

Column 1	Column 2	Column 3	Column 4
criticism	obligations	nightmares	performing
freedom	feelings	friends	pets
trips	worries	fights	injustice
current events	homework	punishment	tattling
grades	vacation	hobbies	drugs
clothes	food	smoking	violence
sex	basketball (sports)	music	buying gifts
co-ed teams	budget crunch	allowances	brothers
divorce	death	guilt	sisters
parents	smart/dumb	spending	KKK
greed	race	expectations	rules
love	behavior	religion	self worth
handicaps	stuff toys	hate	body changes
pressure	economy (money)	yelling	mistakes
achievement	success	achievement	movie stars
cosmetics	winning	illnesses	careers
anger	hair styles	courtesy	fantasy
dancing	indifference	boredom	awareness
abortion	exercise	daydreaming	laughter
bravery	fairness	imagination	poetry
creativity	jokes	crying	moving
war	patriotism	bullies	energy
hunger	risk taking	time	population
sleep overs	pain	draft	adventure
cheating	conversation	exploration	copying
hope	solo parents	stealing	television
shoplifting	lying	vandalism	cooperation
flowers	ownership	goals	tests
free time	sharing time	SRA	future
being liked	insects	guns	showing love
loneliness	older people	babies	overweight
killing animals	being hurt	spanking	bribery
dieting	being alone	braces	
gambling	retention	dating	
	saving	relatives	

Figure 3.   Topics for Open Class Meetings at the Franklin School

Areas That Went Well:
   1.
   2.
   3.
Areas That Showed Need For Revision:
   1.
   2.
   3.
Date of Discussion: **Name:**
   1. I thought today's discussion was:
   2. The thing that interested me most in today's discussion was:
   3. I think we spent too much time in:
   4. It would have helped me more if:
   5. What I'm willing to do about 3 and 4 is:
   6. The things we talked about were:
      insignificant 1 2 3 4 5 6 7 8 9 very significant
   7. During the session I was:
      uninvolved 1 2 3 4 5 6 7 8 9 very involved
   8. Please comment on any issue related to the group, the class or today's discussion. (Use the back of the sheet if necessary.)

Figure 4. Open Meeting—Teacher, Student Evaluation

Individual or types of small group follow up is determined by the amount of time, depth, and the type of investigative work required. Minimal time and depth investigation, focused on accumulating already existing information and requiring minimal investigation, is best done by individuals. When multiple sources are to be used and specific information recorded with minimal interpretation required, pairs or triads are well suited to do the work.

When the investigative work requires critical thinking and problem solving, cooperative groups become the mechanism for the investigative endeavor. Cooperative groups, due to the time and complexity of creating and managing, should be used specifically to ensure superior product production that requires a correct information base and the need for critical analysis and problem solving. The creation of interdependency in the group is dependent on the need of the group to engage in critical thinking and problem solving. When these two needs are non-existent, the cooperation effort is seldom demonstrated. When cooperative groups become dysfunctional, it's most likely due to the fact the tasks in which they are involved are based on information gathering and could be done more efficiently by basic small work groups or individually.

Process Class Meetings. The third type of class meeting is the process meeting. Following the investigative work of the motivational meeting, the class meeting is reconvened for the purpose of processing the work that has been done. When the investigative work has been done individually or in basic small groups, the information and conclusions drawn may be of the type that doesn't require a process meeting. They may be assignments that will be handed in for teacher assessment, self- or peer-evaluated and may not require total class discussion. If discussion is required, the process class meeting should be convened and a short, direct, information sharing meeting take place.

When the work is done in cooperative groups, it must always be processed in the process class meeting. The facilitating skills for the cooperative group process meeting differ from those used in the open or motivational class meeting, due to the meeting's immediate focus. There is no initial need for definition and personalization, as the purpose is to have each cooperative group present its product. The group presentation is then followed up with the facilitator asking questions focused on the procedures and processes that were used to determine and create the product. The discussion on procedure and process of exploration becomes the primary outcome of the meeting.

Each cooperative group's work assignment must include the need to engage in critical thinking and problem solving. Each group's product must be developed around specific outcome statements that require special information that must be interpreted and then applied for completion of the product. The sharing and analysis of each group's procedure and the specific thinking and problem solving skills that were required to produce the product become the focuses for probing questions.

As the process meeting progresses, the students are continuing to discuss the procedures used to reach the group's conclusion and the necessary thinking and problem solving skills that were utilized. The process meeting questions are analytical in nature and allow for in-depth analysis and peer discovery and the systematic teaching of critical thinking and problem solving is accomplished. The process meeting questions center around the what, why, and how decisions are made.

The reason traditional individualized taught classrooms failed to teach critical thinking and problem solving was due to the isolation of learning. These two skills can only be taught in an interactive environment.

The three different class meetings should not require long periods of time when being employed. Meetings for elementary aged children will normally last ten to fourteen minutes. Middle school students' meetings are twelve to eighteen minutes in length and high school students, twenty minutes. One of the difficult aspects of facilitating open and motivational meetings is to end them when they are on a roll with high energy being released.

Task Groups

There are four task groups: the basic task group, cooperative task group, base group, and the special needs group. The four grouping arrangements constitute the basis for student to student learning. Students are taught that their participation in groups is important and they are expected to cooperate and work hard in whatever capacity constitutes their responsibility.

The basic and cooperative task groups are continually formed as new learning products are needed. The members comprise the team until the product is finished and processed at the process class meeting. Immediately after the processing class meeting is finished, the membership is dismantled and a new membership will be formed when the next need arises. Students are assigned randomly to the task groups and with continual new membership the opportunity for all students to eventually work with one another is guaranteed. Students do not choose their own members for a task group nor are they to complain about the make up of the group membership. They must understand that the teacher is using a randomizing system that is fair when selecting membership for a specific group. The membership continually changes, so whoever makes up the immediate group will change for the next product that needs to be created. The continual mixing of the group members causes student to student appreciation of each other as they work together and share in the accomplishments of production.

The group's size and length of existence depend upon the complexity and depth of the task it is required to perform. Some task groups will meet on a one-time basis, seek out needed information, and reach product standards quickly, while some may be involved for extended periods of time. Product selection, setting standards, developing checkpoints to ensure quality and final self inspection are covered in detail in Chapter 4.

Some tasks are best accomplished by pairs or triads and never should a task group have over four members. When the group make up reaches five or more, it becomes unmanageable as the size of the group becomes cumbersome when needing to set the plan to reach their outcomes. Five or more in a group will normally split into a group of two and a group of three. Then, in each of the two groups, a member evolves as a leader and each begin vying for leadership. The group then splits into two competing sections and allegiance to work as a cohesive group no longer exists. Groups of three or four seldom have this problem and I think it is due to students' sense of fairness— two to one or three to one is viewed as "ganging up." Two on two is positive for critical thinking and problem solving. Triads or groups of four have a likelihood of each member supporting each other and working hard to accomplish the group goals.

The use of specific grouping patterns are designed into the total planning of the lesson and are selected from individualized work, basic task groups or cooperative learning groups. At the completion of the motivational class meeting, one of the patterns will be employed.

The complexity of subject exploration and degree of investigation determines the individual, basic, or cooperative group make up. Some investigative work is best accomplished by individual follow up. When the particular study is short term, requires minimal sources for the information base, requires minimal interpretation, and is completed by following specific directions, individual work is adequate. Fill in the blank, multiple choice, and specific short answer questions that are purely information-based all fall into the individualized follow up categories.

Basic small groups, working for specific information and then needing to put their information together to form a final product, are adequate for the completion of many group learning products. These basic task groups are quickly formed by randomly placing students into triads or foursomes, assigning them specific work responsibilities, such as specific readings, math computation problems, listening to taped messages, and then assigning each individual to draw his or her own conclusions. At the completion of their individual work, they combine their ideas into a team developed product. The basis for the product they are developing is information based and only needs each member to share his or her findings and combine the information. A significant amount of classroom work meets these requirements and should be completed in a basic group structural process with minimal time required.

The cooperative groups, based upon social interaction interdependent information sharing, critical thinking, and problem solving, are more complex to form, manage, and require longer time allotments to reach product completion. It is imperative that the quality managed classroom provide some opportunity for students to learn in cooperative groups, as the teaching of social interaction skills, critical thinking, and problem solving are basic to creating high quality products and are a necessary skill to be successful in life-long learning, work, and personal fulfillment.

There is ample material written on forming and managing cooperative groups. Drs. David and Roger Johnson's research and books are examples of why and how to engage in cooperative learning.

The first factor for successful task group learning is knowing when to use individualized, basic task group, or cooperative task grouping. The majority of classroom learning can be accomplished through structured individualized and basic task group work. Cooperative groups need to be used in specific situations and are effective when the task to be completed requires problem solving and creative thinking. Figure 5 can be used as a means for reflection and evaluation for effective facilitating.

Base Groups

The groups are teacher formed, based upon collected data, starting after the first four to six weeks of the school year, with membership lasting for the entire school year, and have triads or four members per group. When initially formed, the base groups have at least one triad group, as the base group becomes the unit that welcomes a new student into the class. One of the responsibilities of the base group is to go to the office when a new student arrives, introduce him/her to the principal, then to the class. Then individual members take the responsibility to show him/her the school, be on the playground with him/her, go to lunch together, and begin to create an environment of inclusion.

The base groups become a support group for their members. The quality managed classroom provides the structure for students to develop social skills and experience opportunities to discuss and problem solve real-life problems. It is in the small base group, which has established cohesion and trust, that students can talk over problems and have peer assistance to work on solutions. As I experience student to student caring and problem solving, I gain more and more faith in their abilities. The problem in the individualized taught classroom is that it has no structure to develop and exhibit the ability. The membership of the group is kept constant throughout the school year to ensure confidentiality and trust. The non-changing of the membership also teaches the valuable lesson that when there is a problem within our group, we work it out, not get out.

Directions: For each observable skill, check the box that you believe describes the degree to which the skill is evident.

Leadership Skills:	Strong	Some	Not Observed	Not Applicable
Provides simple ground rules				
Selects relevant topics				
Supports, motivates, encourages				
Understands alternate views				
Keeps group on task				
Allows flexibility				
Allows closure with openendedness				
Participants accept direction				

Defining Questions:	Strong	Some	Not Observed	Not Applicable
Limits topic of discussion				
Maintains focus on definition				

Personalizing Questions:	Strong	Some	Not Observed	Not Applicable
Relates topic to participant				
Participant chooses level				

Challenging Questions:	Strong	Some	Not Observed	Not Applicable
Requests clarification				
Encourages examination of assumptions				
Seeks depth, evaluation of ideas				
Provides unusual perspective				
Allows generalizations				

Cohesiveness:	Strong	Some	Not Observed	Not Applicable
Participants share personal experiences				
Participants accept risking				
Discussion flows between participants				
Leader becomes less dominant				
Humor				

Productivity: List group accomplishments on back.

Figure 5. Facilitator Self-Evaluation Form

The individualized classroom, with its emphasis on individualized work, its non-depth involvement of peers, and the message that if you have a problem, academically or socially, you work it out alone, has created an attitude that strong people individually work out their own problems. If it can't be worked out, then just get out. In the workplace, if I'm having a problem with the boss, I quit and get out. In personal relationships, when there is a problem, I just get out. Base group participation teaches the opposite perspective: strong people share their problems and help each other work out solutions. When there is a relating problem, we work it out, not get out.

The students are continually taught throughout the school year that the teacher is always called to the group if any member mentions or talks about being harmed, sexually, physically, or psychologically, or that they might harm themselves or someone else. When the teacher is called to the group, he or she meets one-to-one with the student and determines if the incident should be reported.

I am finding that a significant number of children do report abuse situations to their group. When this happens, usually a member of the group makes the request for the teacher to come to the group. I believe students have the strength to report the situation because they know they have the support of their group. The reporting and teacher involvement do not interfere with the group members' sense of confidentiality or trust and, in most cases, strengthens the bond. Students are never involved in follow-up actions or becoming problem solvers for the individual students. This is handled in strict confidence with the school, social services, and legal authorities.

The base group, once it becomes functional, becomes the place that students learn and develop social skills. I see teachers attempting to use cooperative task grouping as the place to teach social skills. It seldom is successful, as the purpose of the cooperative group is to develop a quality product, and when inappropriate social skills have caused the group to become dysfunctional, production stops. This leaves members that want to be productive feeling frustrated with the inappropriate member and the process of production stopped, and a group member becoming unpopular. The social skills need to be taught elsewhere, in the base groups, where there is a commitment to help each other.

The introduction of basic social skills can be introduced during either open or motivational class meetings. These meetings are then followed up with base group discussions where the skill is personalized. Social skill streaming sequences such as *Skill-Streaming the Elementary School Child* by

Ellen McGinnia and Arnold P. Goldstein are sources to use to determine basic social skills that are appropriate for the different developmental models.

When an individual class member is expressing behavior indicative of an inappropriate social skill, the teacher individually discusses the lack of appropriate behavior with the student and suggests that the base group help him/her learn the appropriate skill. The teacher, with the student, then meets with the base group, explains the need, and enlists the support of the group. The group then becomes the primary skill teaching unit.

The groups are formed after there has been considerable observation and sociograms administered. The first four to six weeks need to be spent gathering the data, to attempt to group the students for the greatest possibility of creating a successful base group (Figure 6). When the groups are formed, control first for the probability of close personal relationships, secondly for diversity. Try to have a gender, socio-economic balance, but do not sacrifice cohesiveness.

Just prior to the forming of the base groups, time needs to be spent teaching the importance and the functions of the base group. This aspect of the formation is extremely important, as the students must sense the enthusiasm and importance that their teacher perceives in base groups. They need to know the confidence the teacher has in their ability to help each other, how important it is to be able to talk and help each other solve problems, and that it is a privilege to be part of a base group. They need to be anticipating the formation of their group.

The procedure following the formation of the groups is to engage members in activities that build personal understanding of each other, communication, trust, and confidence. Have them discuss topics that are fun and noncontroversial, participate in activities that are trust building, and engage in activities that allow students to work together to develop joint products where each member can contribute. Have them come up with a name for their group and a non-verbal signal to greet each other. Each of these outcomes stay confidential to the group so they can begin to build the idea of uniqueness. The activities used to build trust and confidence should not take long periods of time and should be done three times a week for about a month. Once trust and confidentiality have been built, the groups become support and problem solving groups. All students should experience the understandings, support, belonging and help that comes from being part of a cohesive small group and the classroom is the most reasonable place for this experience to happen.

Create a "Base Group Data Gathering" sheet. Specific areas for data gathering are:
1. Who plays with whom
2. Who is selected as peer leaders
3. Who appears to be isolated
4. Who has negotiation skills
5. Who is willing to compromise
6. Who shows empathy
7. Who is a helper
8. Who is sensitive
9. Who is flexible
10. Who is patient
11. Who is organized
12. Who is a talker
13. Who is a listener

Name	Negotiate +/-	Compromise +/-	Empathize +/-	Helper +/-	Sensitive +/-

Name	Flexible +/-	Organizer +/-	Talker +/-	Listener +/-

Figure 6.   Base Group Data Gathering Sheet

Select activities that:

1. Establish a trusting relationship
2. Cause openness and honesty
3. Increase honest, caring, and direct communication
4. Increase self-awareness
5. Cause awareness that others have concerns/problems
6. Increase the individual's ability to care for others
7. Show how to recognize and respect the feelings of others
8. Show how to accept responsibility

The base group can be called to action by the teacher or at the request of any one of its members. The teacher uses the group for discussion of high interest local or national current affairs, general school or classroom social concerns, or teaching of social skills. A group may also be used to assist one of its members for special development and monitoring of a social skill. The teacher seldom is directly involved in the group discussion and understandings but is always available to be called to assist. Action plans are kept to the trust of the group.

The base group can also be used as an integral part of the teaching-learning cycle. The area that often is missing in classroom learning is to take knowledge and understanding to an action plan. This inability to move to an action plan is one of the critical factors that cause learning to be perceived as irrelevant. The base group can often be used as the vehicle for action plans, particularly social actions plans. After the content of a unit has been discussed, conclusions drawn, and understandings developed, the base group can become the place for members to make plans, either individually or as a group, to do something.

I observed a fifth grade teacher use the base groups in the above manner. She has the students participating and learning in a two week science unit titled "Steward of the Environment." The students explored concerns about the environment from world, national, state, and local perspectives and tied the concepts with stewardship. The last thing the teacher did as part of the unit was to call the base groups to action. She told them that they were to become stewards of the school environment and challenged them to discuss and make plans of action. She told them that the plans were theirs and they were not to be shared with her. Throughout the remainder of the year the teacher called the base groups together and had them share on their stewardship and continue to expand or develop new plans. The unit ran the entire school year. Students want a way to do something with the knowledge they are gaining. Base groups work.

Special Needs Groups

The fourth grouping pattern is an empowerment process that arranges for student teaching student. It is used to assist a student that is having difficulty with a specific academic skill.

At the completion of the time allotted for the mastering of a skill and it is obvious the student has not mastered the skill, an individual conference is called. The conference is initiated by the teacher who shares his/her concern regarding the need for mastery of the skill and their perception of the student's present level of mastery. The teacher does not threaten the student nor place his/her values pertaining to the need for mastery. The conference is straightforward.

The student is then asked to share his/her perception of how well he/she has mastered the skill and it usually coincides with the teacher's perception. When the discussion reaches this understanding, it becomes evident that the student had taken verbal ownership of not mastering the skill.

The teacher then asks if the student would want to continue to work toward mastery and explains that the majority of class members will be moving toward the mastery of another skill, often dependent upon the skill just learned. At this point, the student is asked to make a judgment regarding his/her desire to work toward mastery. If he/she expresses the wish to continue to work on the skill, it is a genuine desire, as they are expressing their own value based upon their seeing the need for mastery.

There are no teacher threats, no punishment, no demands. Students normally express a wanting to be better at the skill. When this is the case, the teachers ask the student to pick two classmates that they think would be willing and able to help them. Students are excellent at picking the right helpers and their request needs to be honored. The teacher then asks the student if he/she could intervene and individually meet with each of the students that were picked. It is explained that the two who were picked may have other needs that would not allow them to have time to help and if that happens they will pick another.

The meeting is to inform the chosen that they have been picked by the student needing help. The skill needing mastery is explained and they are asked if they would like to assist the student. The anticipated helpers are asked to evaluate their own ability to help and assess their other responsibilities to see if they have time to help and the teacher will provide time for them to help as well as help them with ideas. If they decide they cannot be effective, another student is selected. Seldom does a helper not respond to the request as the sense of importance that is gained is extreme and most often the helpers are anxious to begin assisting.

The teacher then arranges time for the triad to work on the skill and is available to meet with the teaching team for the developing of teaching strategies or to answer questions they might have.

The students work together whenever there are slack moments in the school day or when assignments are finished early, sometimes at recess or shortened noon hour playground time if they so desire. The student working toward skill mastery continues to participate in the new skill development with the rest of the class in an attempt not to fall too far behind.

The four grouping patterns become major factors that create connectiveness for quality classroom management. They provide a variety of classroom learning arrangements that emphasize quality relationships and quality academic outcomes.

4

Inspection to Self-Assessment

INSPECTION MODEL—THE PROBLEM

Whenever I am looking to purchase an item and it has a label attached to it stating "Inspected by," I am immediately on guard. If the product was quality, there would be no need for the "inspector" mentality. However, we have been exposed so long to a model of production that has inspectorship as the definition of quality that we have accepted it as the hallmark.

As the inspectorship mentality has dictated American schooling and industry, we have witnessed a decrease in quality of work. It has been demonstrated by numerous publications that American standards of quality in education and industry are inferior when compared on a world basis. Where is the root of this problem? Is it in a lost pride of workmanship? Is it our capitalist system that evolves around mass production, with the acceptance that quantity has priority over quality? Is it the management-worker relationship where the boss assumes to have the power to make workers produce? Is it that as consumers we are willing to purchase inferior products if the price is right? Or, is it caused by having lost the ability to set a standard that requires quality? I fear it may well be the result of a schooling process being imposed upon learners for thirteen years, the developmental years, which breeds acceptance of all of the above. When one examines the assessment model in our schools, which is taught at teacher training institutions, it is obviously one of inspection. The model promotes the teacher as having total and final authority over quality. This is the outcome when the product is evaluated solely on an outsider's point of reference. The problem of inspection is twofold. The inspector becomes the standard setter and the evaluation process inhibits the teacher from being perceived as a helper.

59

In universities, the student's job is to create predefined products. Produce the paper, take the test, practice the lesson plan, etc., while the professor plays out the role of inspector. His/her job is to define the product, set the standard, and inspect/evaluate the product by assigning his/her indicator of quality. The future teacher has already been conditioned to the inspectorship model by thirteen years of public school evaluation and is now further programmed to perpetuate the system.

I do not believe the problem rests solely on the teachers; it's the problem of how teachers have been subjected to a system that emulates inspection. How can they be expected to perform outside of the inspection model when they have been molded by it and are expected to enforce it? Yet, the possibility to reverse the role of inspectorship is now in our grasp. We have a model that can move the classroom from outside evaluation to one of self evaluation and, in the process, create the environment for quality work. Outside evaluation, in managerial language, is "top-down" whereas self-evaluation is "bottom-up."

Inspection exemplifies top down management and implies that quality will be produced as the consequence of the outside "expert." This is the role that has been assigned and accepted by teachers. Bottom-up management is based upon the premise that the person or persons producing the product have a basic desire to produce quality work and are the most reasonable and qualified ones to make the final decision regarding quality. The student needs to be empowered and taught the skills of self-assessment and have the final decision as to the quality of their products.

There is confusion in educational thinking as to what constitutes which type of management. Dr. Glasser, in the preface of his book titled *The Quality School*, quotes Shayle Uroff in an attempt to differentiate the boss manager (top-down) from the lead manager (bottom-up):

A boss drives.	A manager leads.
A boss relies on authority.	A manager creates confidence.
A boss says "I."	A manager says "we."
A boss creates fear.	A manager shows how.
A boss creates resentment.	A manager breeds enthusiasm.
A boss fixes blame.	A manager fixes mistakes.
A boss makes work drudgery.	A manager makes work interesting.

Through these two different managerial techniques, we can see the possibility for two very different outcomes in terms of student quality and output.

The top-down teacher drives, authoritates, and uses fear, resentment, and blame in an atmosphere of drudgery. No teacher intentionally practices these things—they are simply part of the cause and effect relationship of top down management. The bottom-up management leads, exhibits confidence in self and others, shows how, and makes learning interesting.

The confusion we see is based on the fact that few teachers understand or realize that inspection automatically creates an environment which does not foster quality work. No teachers believe they use coercive techniques in their classroom. Everyone becomes a bottom up manager in theory, but not in practice. Ask a teacher who views her/himself as a lead manager and ask if he/she uses rewards and punishments, a preset grading system, predetermined lesson plans, pre-established rules, and more often than not he/she will respond: "Of course, I do—how else do you run a classroom?"

The following characteristics taken from educational periodicals and described as indicators of bottom up management verify this confusion of what constitutes top down, bottom up management.

These six principles are reported to be the prime factors that create a learning environment where the student has a greater amount of on-task engaged time, which reports increased learning. The term *effective lead manager* is often used to describe the teacher who implements the principles.

1. Planning—before school year (materials, space, rules, procedures); daily plans posted.
2. Room is arranged for ease of mobility and eye contact.
3. System and procedures for class activities are taught to students at the beginning of the year.
    Transitions
    Distribution of materials
    Homework
    Recess
    Using the restroom
    Sharpening pencils
    Question-answer sessions
    Beginning class on time
    What to do when work is finished
4. Directions are clear.
5. Active teaching includes a variety of activities, lots of teacher-led instruction with less set work.
6. Monitoring occurs during set work, and interactions are short (precise, prompt, and leave).

When one analyzes these six points, it becomes obvious that we are discussing top-down management. The six points all refer to teacher-planned, teacher-driven learning. The teacher is in charge, all procedures and progress are pre-determined, and the student becomes the recipient completely denied the possibility of ownership and decision making regarding their classroom. Re-read the six points and it becomes obvious they are the products of a top-down managed classroom.

My grandson in elementary school brought home his material and procedure list at the end of the first day. It stated he should have one pink eraser. When he and his mother went shopping, they found a blue eraser, as well as a pink one. After a discussion, Zack decided to buy the blue one, to see if his teacher would react to his choice. He came home the next day and reported blue instead of pink didn't seem to make any difference to the teacher, but his classmates told him that he simply must go buy a pink one right away. Top down management destroys creativity, involvement, taking chances, choice making, decision making, and ownership, and promotes conformity.

Inspection becomes the vehicle which the top-down manager uses in an attempt to achieve quality, even though it fails to do so. The concepts of self-responsibility, self-determination, self-assessment, and "we work together" are of little or no consequence. Because this model of boss management is continually modeled and systematically taught to education majors, it becomes the system perpetuated by most school systems. It becomes very difficult for a teacher, a particular school within a system or the system itself to perform outside this model!

Cooperative learning, one of the major positive movements in classroom teacher delivery, even falls into the trap of inspection. The teacher is taught to do small group monitoring, oftentimes interpreted as the need to use frequent positive verbal reinforcement to keep the group on task or to become quickly involved to redirect the group when it begins to go off task. For cooperative learning to be truly effective, task groups must verbally reinforce or correct themselves during on-task time. The teacher's role is to watch the students for later discussion, but not to intervene in any way. One of the most difficult re-training steps for a teacher to progress through (to become an effective teacher of cooperative learning) is to not continually intervene during the time the task groups are working; it's hard to break the inspection habit.

I find major problems within the inspection model itself. As I wrote before, it is built upon the outside evaluator which creates situations and attitudes that are detrimental to the students' perceptions of self and school and are equally destructive to the overall classroom environment. Inspection implies more than grading student work and filling in a report card. It inherently implies total teacher responsibility for all aspects of the classroom, including behavior management, rules and regulations, and motivational techniques. These will be discussed in detail in Chapter 5 on creating a noncoercive classroom. Inspectorship mentality denies the student the opportunity to be a significant decision maker regarding his/her own learning and behavior. Inspectorship management, which places the teacher in complete charge, becomes overwhelming and energy exhaustive and creates an adverse teacher/student relationship.

The system of inspectorship sets in place the model for students to do low quality work. This is partially accomplished by students developing an attitude and behaviors of doing just enough to succeed, based upon the students' degree of concern over which A–F grade they receive. There is little difference between the "A" and "D" student regarding attitude toward work. Both have developed the attitude of doing only what needs to be done to meet the inspector's requirements. The "A" student will do more work to get the "A" grade, but seldom goes beyond the assigned work. The "D" student does less work with the attitude of just enough to get by.

A second aspect of inspectorship that is detrimental to student attitude of doing high quality work results from negative feedback. The inspector's job is to evaluate, give feedback, and require re-doing to meet the standards.

I'm sure all can remember the time (or times) in our elementary or secondary school career when a paper was returned to us thoroughly inspected. It had as many teacher evaluation marks as our own writing. These evaluation marks meant either a failure or the dreaded "do over" syndrome. If you were fortunate enough to receive only a few of these marked inspected papers, then you were a student who had the skills that were being expected, understood the system, and agreed to work within the system. Most likely you did, as you made it through the inspection system for at least sixteen years with a fair amount of success and minimal discomfort. However, many students didn't make it or they appeared to make it when in all honesty they hadn't. For them, the marked up papers, the repeated failures, and the endless do overs all equated one of two meanings. Either they believed they were incompetent in that subject area, and thus gave up, or they believed they couldn't succeed because their teacher didn't like them and therefore wouldn't let them. Both of these responses are absolutely devastating to a student and should be inconceivable classroom outcomes from a teacher's perspective.

When I discuss the issue of inspection with elementary age school children, the majority view negative evaluation reports as the result of their inability to grasp the concepts. Once they form the perception (usually during, if not before, the third grade) that the problem is within them (they have failed due to not being able), their enthusiasm for the subject begins to diminish. This is followed by a decreased amount of energy allotted to the subject, which creates a downward spiral. This perception of "I can't do the work" is then continually reinforced by the inspection model.

I often hear many well-intentioned teachers attest to the fact that they cannot expect the same levels of work from one student as from another, while they continue to grade, evaluate, and inspect all students through the same standard and system. It doesn't take long for the student who receives poor evaluation marks to see him/herself as a failure in subjects where he/she gets low marks. The student assumes the problem causing the low marks is his/her fault as he/she observes others doing well. Such a student quickly learns to dread the time given to his/her "weak" subject, creates a state of fear, frustration, and confusion, and begins to develop strategies to avoid the subject. The student rejects all that the subject entails, refuses to do required work, and is punished for it. Thus, the perception is continually solidified. The downward spiral is totally intact and strengthened by many of the teacher's behaviors, which are the outcome of the inspectorship model.

By the time students are in middle school, many subjects are rejected completely. I am annoyed and frustrated by this rejection of subject matter, but when investigating as to why, I'm never surprised when they say that they didn't make the inspector's grade. How can anyone twelve years old dislike the sciences, with all of its mysteries, excitement, revelations; or math and its relations to logic (not withstanding the fact that it is used everyday) or any of the other subjects taught in middle school? In each area, if the student doesn't like it, I can guarantee you, one of the major reasons is she/he didn't make the grade. The only difference is by now approximately ten percent of the students have been weeded out by special education and the majority of the rest have discovered numerous ways to beat the system and minimize the pains of failure and hard work. The inspector model has eliminated a personal standard of quality, and the inspector standard is now ignored.

When discussing inspection with high school students, their perception changes dramatically. Many see the problem of inspectors as a personality conflict: the teacher simply doesn't like me. She/he has favorites that get the good grades and no matter how hard I try, she/he sees me as a "C" student.

Quickly they report "Why try?" Another common response is: "I'll do just enough to get by; it really doesn't matter how hard I try." When talking with high school teachers, the most common concern I hear is: "What can we do to get them to work? They just don't seem to care." The major problem in the high schools today is the students' unwillingness to work hard in the academic areas, and this problem is inherited by high school teachers. Motivation through inspection was so misused in the earlier years that by high school, for many students, work is a non-existent aspect of school life.

In the primary and intermediate grades, if the students perceive themselves as good, it's due to the fact that the teacher, acting in the inspector role, has granted them good reports. The student response has been a self-perception that, first of all, "I'm good at this," and secondly, "The teacher likes me." This student, when in high school, continues to work and relate and is productive. When the opposite happens and the inspector issues bad reports, the response is, "I'm not good at this subject and I'm not liked by teachers, so why try." There are too many students that have the "I don't care" and "It really doesn't matter" attitudes *before* they enter high school. This tragic attitude then continues throughout high school and becomes the norm in adulthood. The consequences are poor self-concept, poor work ethics, and the willingness to accept a standard of producing low quality work.

INSPECTION TO SELF-ASSESSMENT

According to the Deming Management Method, "Companies that depend on mass inspection to guarantee quality will never improve quality. Inspections are too late, unreliable and ineffective" (Walton, p. 92).

Now, substitute the word "school" for companies: "Schools that depend on mass inspection to guarantee quality will never improve quality. Inspections are too late, unreliable, and ineffective."

Can the classroom teacher function effectively without doing some inspection? No! The answer lies in developing a balance between teacher input (determined by the student) and student self-assessment as the quality control process for the completion of a quality learner product. Thus, we begin to create a definition of inspection based upon student determination rather than teacher inspection. This concept rests on the belief that true and lasting motivation is intrinsic. The student self-assessment model is built upon the premise of trust—that all students want to perform well, interact, become engaged in learning, and continually seek new and higher levels of performance, thus continually improving the quality of their work. The research on motivation consistently reports that for work to be meaningful and done at a high level of quality, it must be personally rewarding, by allowing for maximum personal input and resulting in personal satisfaction. This finding is a reflection of how and why we choose all of our behavior. What motivates us to behave is our wanting to fulfill basic needs and wants. These needs and wants are self-perceived and expressed by needing to have fun, freedom, belonging, and power. When we encourage students to become self-assessors we begin the process of the opening of these power pathways by teaching them the process of self-determination. They become the people who have the power to determine what aspect of a lesson they will become involved in, the degree of involvement they want, what the final products will be, and the degree of quality they will emulate.

In the inspection model, there is an assumed expectancy placed on classroom teachers to be responsible for the production of work that their students do. Most often this expectation is created through a combination of the principal's expectations, the result of their teacher preparation, and assumed parent expectation. With these expectations, the attitude of needing to be in charge to keep order and engineer the learning process of students is quite logical. The belief that "I'm responsible personally for causing learners to learn a given amount of information in a nine month period" is reflected over and over again when teachers talk with each other. This perception also becomes enmeshed in the opposite direction. Not only do they need to prepare their students for the next academic school year, but they also must adjust to the perceived failures of last years' teachers to prepare the students for *this* school year. All of us who teach have been engaged in the discussion which reflects that "why hasn't someone before me done their job?" issue. In the inspection model, the teacher, as well as the student, can never add up, never "win," and therefore, never create an environment of quality.

I was scheduled to observe a student teacher in a kindergarten class and when I entered the room the regular classroom teacher was verbally engaged with the children. She was so focused she didn't see me enter. By the tone of her voice and the direct message that "everyone of you had better settle down and get to work" I thought she was preparing them for a good performance with the student teacher (for my benefit) during the observations. But she wasn't; she went on to inform them how hard first grade would be and how much was going to be expected of them. She weighed this against how poorly, in her opinion, they were doing to get ready for first grade. As she put the fear of first grade into their internal world, I could see her own sense of accomplishment reflected by the little people sitting there—mouths open, eyes big, and listening to every word. I wasn't surprised when the student teacher used the same procedure during her lesson.

After the observation, we had a three way conversation regarding the lesson I had observed. When I inquired about the motivational technique of using fear for first grade, both the classroom teacher and the student teacher became somewhat offended and informed me that their job is to prepare students for first grade. Because of their obvious frustration with me, I decided not to ask them how preparation for the rigors of the first grade had outweighed the psychological and academic levels of the kindergartners' own needs. They then proceeded to let me know just how little I know about the issue of "teacher accountability," which meant that they were ineffective teachers in the eyes of the principal if they were unable to prepare kindergartners for the next school year. I realized that the inspection model was well in place in that particular school and classroom and that we were preparing a new teacher to emulate the same model.

Why do classroom teachers perform in an inspection model program? They have been immersed in the theory and practice of behaviorism. They believe that as classroom teachers, they are responsible for all learning; the most effective way to get results is to use a combination of rewards and punishments which establish the teacher's sense of control and power, causing the student to become dependent upon the teacher. The teacher accomplishes this through inspecting and making judgment regarding student produced work and behavior.

Once this inspectorshipping has been internalized, the logical follow up belief is the teacher is responsible for and should know what the students should learn and the rate at which the learning needs to happen. The standard can now be set, and it is a standard based upon the average of the group. Now, as the teacher inspects the student's individual performance, the teacher not only judges the student's work, but the teacher can also judge the student. If the student's performance doesn't match the standard, it's not the teacher's fault; there must be something wrong with the student. Thus, teachers sort and then create the many levels of education as inspection continues, justified by new standardized criteria. These levels keep expanding: from gifted and talented to regular education to alternative education to exceptional education, to specializations in special education, to levels within the specialized area of exceptional education; they never stop.

This mind set is so enmeshed in our thinking that we have national and state educational departments that actually believe we can change individual student performance by simply re-establishing a new standard that has higher expectations. We are then forced to do more inspection by the incorporation of state and national testing programs. It is a vicious, destructive, downward spiral and the individual child in the classroom suffers the consequences.

Dr. Deming so emphatically points out in his seminars on management method that as the worker in the American industrial model is degraded and manipulated into a lesser degree of control over his/her dignity on the job, the pride of work and output equally disintegrates. A sense of disenchantment, hopelessness, and eventually apathy become the consequences of degradation and manipulation. Such a sequence is so often spoken of by teachers and echoed by students.

Standards are an absolute necessity in the production of quality work. As was emphasized in the first two chapters, students must be continually involved in classroom discussion, modeling, and analyzing quality. A major aim of the classroom teacher is to have all students develop an awareness of standards of quality and to assist them as they learn the process of setting high, yet reasonably accomplished, standards for their work. Standards have meaning when they become self-determined and self-assessed.

How do we move away from our present mode of inspection to self-assessment? We can't until we change our belief system about how we behave and are motivated. I alerted you to the fact that a prerequisite to this book is *The Quality School* written by Dr. William Glasser, published by Harper and Row, 1990. If you have read the book, go back and reread chapters 4, 5, and 6. If you haven't read the book, do so now.

When is inspection needed? Dr. Deming advocates that it is of absolute necessity during the period that the product is being produced. It is what happens during the process of production that creates quality, not the inspection of the finished product. The students must be taught how to program the teacher into their quality management process by using him/her for feedback during the creation of the product, which enables them to reach the high level of quality that has been predetermined and articulated. Inspection has as its only purpose helping the students to gain confidence and progress toward the degree of quality that satisfies their final self-assessment of the product.

This is very different from collecting the work at the end of the designated time of completion and proceeding to make the final judgment about the value of the work. A curricula that comes closest to continual feedback with minimal final teacher evaluation is art. Seldom does one observe students not working in art, and there is an excitement about what they are doing. The art teacher is continually moving about the students, often stopping and talking with them about a specific aspect of their creation, sometimes suggesting a perspective, but seldom telling them they have to do it differently. The final product is usually self-evaluated. A very different picture emerges in what are considered the basic subject matter classes such as language, math, social studies, and science. The students are normally engaged in teacher directed work, oftentimes by specific questions from a workbook, either teacher made or textbook designed; the teacher is the supervisor, or boss manager, and the students understand that the work will be turned in for teacher inspection. Give students the option of math class or art and most will choose art. Most students respond that art is fun and math is not.

As teachers we need to analyze why art is more fun, and then the factors of creativity, ownership, and self-motivation become apparent. I do not believe that it is the subject itself which is fun or not, but it is the student's personal belief and level of control over the process and outcomes that cause it to be a pleasurable or non-pleasurable experience.

The students will need to be taught and have continual assistance as they perfect the process of becoming proficient self-assessors. It is impossible for them to make this transition unaided, and much confusion and frustration often occur as students set out to redefine evaluation and set their own standards of quality. This is quite normal, especially for students who have spent years in the traditional system of teacher directed assignments and outcomes.

Teachers need to realize that pure self-assessment is most appropriate for topical study in areas of science, social studies, health issues, problem solving, literature, writing, the performing areas of art, physical education, music, and technical education. Each topic or unit is a unit of study that has specific knowledge, attitude development, and action plans of personal implementation (Figure 7, page 78). They provide opportunity for individual exploration, individual standard setting, and creation of different products to express the outcomes. Topical units allow for maximum variability. Skill building in the areas of reading and math are sequential and more defined. They are teacher directed, specifically taught, and need documentation of mastery, as future skills are dependent upon the initial mastery. The student must have minimal variation of performance in these two areas.

Assessment in these two skill building areas involves demonstration of mastery of a skill. Oftentimes self-assessment is focused toward record keeping that reflects mastery of specific skills and documentation of application of skills such as numbers of books read, comments about the books, and who they were read to with confirmation by assigned listeners. This area of self-assessment record keeping lends itself well to individual computerized programs which will be highly motivational in themselves. Each stu- dent needs to have his/her own disk, record book, or portfolio and do the most simplified self-assessment procedure or recording (Figure 8, page 79-80).

The process of teaching and applying true self-assessment in the topical areas has five basic steps.

1. Determination of what, how, and depth of inquiry
2. Definition of product
3. Setting standards
4. Benchmarking
5. Final assessment

Determination of What, How, and Depth of Inquiry

The first step occurs during introduction of the lesson and is part of the motivation. It is to help the students realize that the topic has different possibilities of exploration, areas for in-depth investigation, or related study, and there is a variety of ways to gain the knowledge. Teaching students to determine what and how they want to learn is the beginning for invested learning that leads to self-assessment and high quality work. The better they can identify the "what to learn," the easier it becomes to determine the "how to learn." The teacher develops the unit and individual lesson plans by referencing the overall source and academic outcomes. These outcomes need to be thoroughly understood by the learner as they become the context in which the student's individual learning action plan is developed. It is a good idea to have the outcomes posted after they have been explained and discussed by the student. At the beginning of the unit, the teacher's enthusiasm and importance for learning about the topic are paramount and directly transfer to the student's interest and enthusiasm to become involved and then engaged in study.

The unit of study has listed a number of areas for student in-depth study and each area is then explained to the student. This explanation is then followed up by the teacher sharing what they will be responsible for as the unit progresses.

When teachers are going to use direct teacher lecture material and what will be highlighted—films, basic reading, assignments, guest lectures, field trips—all is outlined. As the students understand what the teacher will be providing and the areas for in-depth study, they begin to plan to develop their "learning action plan." The teacher needs to set parameters such as time allotted for inquiry and product development and time for specific product presentation. This definition of teacher and student responsibilities is basic to developing quality learning and quality work.

Definition of Product

The second step is to help the students understand the need to define their product. The students do not complete assignments or develop projects as they are taught the language of quality management, which centers on product development. The product that is to be produced must relate to the outcomes of the unit of study and is viewed as an integral part of the unit, not something that is done as extra credit. They need to understand that their product will be used to help all of their classmates inrease their knowledge and understanding regarding the area of study and they will present their product to their classmates. It can be a picture, a report, an oral presentation, a video, an authority to speak on the topic, or whatever it is that the students believe will help them in the process of developing a knowledge base and making application of the information. I am always amazed at the variation of products created when the students are given the opportunity to choose their products. The products often correlate with each student's perceived individual learning style. The writers often write, talkers often speak, the scientist develops an experiment, and the dramatist creates a skit.

Another thing that never ceases to surprise me is the confidence they have to experiment with different products. As they watch, listen, and interact with their peers who are experimenting with various modes of expression to solidify their learning, they see new ways to learn themselves. How different this is: no more "take out your work books, open to page twenty, do questions one through nine, try to have it done by the end of the period, if not take it home and have it ready to be checked by the beginning of class tomorrow." Quality learning is different.

Setting the Standards of Quality

The third step of self-assessment is to set the personal standard of quality that the product will possess. The standards of quality become the criteria that sets the parameters of the product and determines the work load. The more exact the individual student or work team is, the more focused they become as they engage in the process for completion of the product. This enables the student to complete the job of self-assessment. The more set standards that are stated, the simpler the final self-assessment task becomes. The more the picture of the product is defined, the clearer the plan of how to proceed.

The standards of the product need to include a description of the final product time variables regarding amount of time for presentation, length of written reports, time of completion of the product, types and numbers of sources of information, and materials needed.

Benchmarking

They must be taught that there must be feedback during the process of production, benchmarks to insure the final product will be quality. This is where the student is taught the principle of going upstream to build quality into the process of development that will ensure a final product that emulates quality. The more exact this criteria is, the more assurance the students have of high quality at completion of their work. The benchmarks need to be identified by stating who will do the inspection, when it will be done, and what feedback, specific information is needed.

I observed two university sophomores attempting to learn the skills of self-assessment in a child development class where I was the teacher. It was entirely new to them, so we had to work through their trauma of not being told what to do to please the teacher while still hoping to receive a high mark. This took some doing, with frustration being expressed through anger and the statement: "You're supposed to tell us what to do." Why wouldn't they think this way when it is how they have worked for the last fourteen years? Teacher tells me what to do, and I do it. Teacher inspects it, assigns me a grade, and I go on to the next assignment. Real simple: all I have to do is complete the assignment the way the teacher wants me to and meet his/her requirements. No need for me to determine what I want to learn, how I want to learn, or to set individual standards. When the final product is done, there is no need to assess it for quality.

Once the students got over the traditional teacher driven instruction, they became quite excited about the idea of self-assessing and developing benchmarks to insure quality. The topic related to television and did it or did it not affect the values of nine- and ten-year-olds. One of the students, based on her perception of being a good writer, decided to develop her product into a written handout of approximately three pages in length. The second, again based on her perception of having strength in oral presentations, planned to develop her product around a four minute speech. Step two was completed—the product was defined.

They then engaged in step three—developing the standards for their finished product. They decided to each watch three different children's television shows and record what values were being presented. They then would meet with each other and compare notes. The notes were shared, they would develop a questionnaire and then interview four nine- or ten-year-olds. They would have designed questions to determine what TV shows were watched and ascertain if they had any effect on these children's values. The last aspect of the investigation was centered on each reading two recently published articles that pertained to the inquiry and see if their findings compared or contradicted their conclusions. It was exciting to watch them set the standards for the development of the final product.

At this point, they set their benchmark for quality checks during the process to ensure that quality is being built into the product and will be achieved upon completion of the work. This is a time that inspection is justifiable as the student has built the inspection into the plan to ensure quality. The two sophomores asked if I would meet with them and look over a rough draft of the questionnaire, check point No. 1, before final submission of the paper and prior to the oral report, would I read and listen and provide specific suggestions, check point No. 2. They asked that I become part of the process at the specific check points and that I do some inspection work.

Helping students understand the need to set specific benchmark points to guarantee quality work can be difficult, especially with primary students. I was discussing this aspect with a first grade teacher. She related how her students interpreted it to mean that they had to have continual monitoring and confirmation of their progress. She found that art was a good area to begin the process of teaching self-assessment, as the students seemed to accept art as being self-directed, individualized, and a personal creation. The students found it easy to talk about the process of creating their pieces of art. She would write the sequential steps which taught them to see the relationships between planning, pre-determined set standard levels, and the need for self-evaluation of their pictures.

The process of becoming self-assessors is developmental. When students have the opportunity to experiment and develop self-assessment skills in the primary grades, they become very proficient by fourth grade. Fourth graders have developed a level of reading, writing, and math skills that give them the latitude to interrelate topical study and academic skills, as well as having the confidence of self-direction that is basic to self-assessment.

Documentation and Evaluation of the Standards

The fifth step of self-assessment is final evaluation, which is determining the degree that the pre-set standards are met and quality of the finished product. Documentation is provided through implementation of a form that has the stated pre-determined set of standards. This includes time of completion, degree of investment of energy, specific references, initial or comments of input persons, and comments of worker regarding understanding of needed information. The final product is dependent on the skill and age level of the student, is talked through with the teacher, or has a written evaluation. Most students, as they are taught the process and become familiar with self-assessment and have it as part of their continual development through school, find the final evaluation quite easy. They eventually realize that quality doesn't just happen. It requires the definition of a product, the predetermined standards, the necessary checkpoint to insure quality, and the need to do a final self-inspection to see that all points have been done. Quality is the mark of their final products.

The student understands that all products must be re-done if they don't meet their quality standards at completion. This assurance, "You have time to redo the product well," is one of the factors that proves the teacher is committed to quality. The student realizes that they don't have to rush and do superficial work to get the job finished. They are being taught to set reasonable expectations within a reasonable time line. Their ability to manage time for product completion is one of the valuable lessons of self directed, self-assessed work.

When helping students develop the idea and standard for a quality product, it is often helpful for them to see some models. Start collecting these models early and get them from other sources, as you don't want to present classmates' work as the model of quality. I have seen this done in classrooms and it sets the stage for unhealthy interactions. It puts the student whose work is exhibited as quality in an awkward and uncomfortable position. They have to deny their good work if they choose to stay as one of the accepted people in the class or they must take on the role of the star. Neither one leads to a positive self concept.

Using small groups to set the standards for self-assessment can also be very effective. The following was given to me and I quote it, but do not know the source:

Small group sessions, where students pool their collective wisdom and devise lists which can be used as guidelines for self-assessment, can play a major role in assisting individual students to decide on their own standard of quality. For example, if you want students to become more aware of the var- ious editing skills they need to use, you might ask the class to work in groups to devise lists of all the editing issues you can think of. Students working on the task in a fifth grade classroom recently included these state-ments:

1. Pull a full stop at the end of a sentence (C.).
2. Put a capital at the start of a sentence or a name (L).
3. Put speech marks when someone talks (" ").
4. Put a question mark after a question (?).
5. If there are two meanings, put brackets around one ([ ]).
6. Put an explanation mark if someone talks loud (!).
7. When you talk about something different start a new paragraph.
8. Commas are for instead of writing "and" (Beverly, Louis, Craig and Jason).
9. This is a sentence _____ (I am sick.).
10. A colon (:) is when you are going to say something but in different words.

Each individual student then worked from the list and developed his/her own list for use when editing the final written products.

Self-assessment isn't easy when it is asked of students who are in high school or university studies when it has not been part of their elementary and secondary school learning experiences. The following is taken from the cover of a graduate student paper written to me in a class that was experiencing self-assessment:

As this is the first time that I have had to self-assess, I must admit that I feel uncomfortable doing it. Not so much as assessing the work but consciously giving myself a mark as how I see my own work and having someone else know how I feel about my work, it's kind of like bragging. However, I honestly feel in this paper I have met the criteria in a sufficient manner, and relating it to my two previous papers, I give myself an A. (I really would have given myself a B so I didn't feel like I was being presumptuous, but I feel really that it is worth an A.)

—Leni

SPECIFIC EXAMPLES OF STUDENT SELF-ASSESSMENT

I. Student Development Contracts

Contract sets the academic expectations and responsibilities for the student as she/he enters into an agreement with the teacher. The contract sets specific tasks that both parties agree upon and for completion within a given period of time. The contract (1) poses problems of varying degrees of difficulty, (2) specific work experience to solve the problems (reading—interview—writing—discussion), (3) benchmark feedback, (4) specific time line, and (5) plan for final evaluation.

II. Student Developed Oral Interviews

The student develops the format for a structured or unstructured dialogue that reflects specific knowledge or understanding gained from specific learning. The student specifies (1) who the interview(s) will be conducted with (peers—adults—experts), (2) develop specific questions to test or receive feedback on knowledge, understanding, (3) sets criteria for questions, (4) provides for benchmarks, (5) sets time line, and (6) criteria for final evaluation.

III. Student Developed Written Interviews

Use same format as #II.

IV. Peer Report/Group Evaluation

The student develops a written oral form that elicits peer responses regarding specific knowledge gained, general understanding, application of knowledge or understanding, participation. The format requires the student analyze self reported peer evaluation by (1) determining the sample, (2) developing specific questions that reflect her/his knowledge, understanding of subject matter, (3) developing benchmarks for quality, (4) setting time line, (5) planning for compilation of data, (6) reporting of data, and (7) planning for assessment of individual learning and peer learning.

V. Portfolios

A collection of student-produced artifacts that serves as evidence of proficiency. The student chooses items that provide samples of specific knowledge gained and application of knowledge. Dates of all work are recorded as well as the facts if the work was the result of individual or group process. The portfolio features accomplishments only, reflects individual learning styles, provides evidence of performance beyond factual knowledge, and depicts the process of learning. The student can select to center the portfolio around specific purposes; examples include area career center portfolio, an achievement portfolio, an assessment portfolio. The student must (1) determine the purpose of the portfolio, (2) set standards for entries, (3) develop a time line, and (4) plan for final self-evaluation of the portfolio.

VI. Student Self-Evaluation of Products

Student products represent completed student work in a variety of forms; written, videotapes, audiotapes, computer demonstrations, dramatic performances, bulletin boards, debates, designs and inventions, investigation reports, simulations, art, physical constructions. Students demonstrate understanding, originality, ability to report progress in an effective and attractive manner, growth in social and academic skills and attitudes and success in meeting criteria. The student must (1) select the product, (2) set standards for quality, (3) determine benchmarks, (4) develop a time line, (5) determine final self-evaluation plan.

VII. Student "I Know—I Think—I Will Try or Do" Statement

The student selects and, in written or oral form, states the "I know—I think—I will try or do" statement. The purpose is to give the student the opportunity to self select things they have learned during a class session, an investigation, or a series of lessons. They accumulate the statements in a series of summary sheets that reflect the student self-analysis of what were important topics, ideas, skills, knowledge, understanding, and applications. The student must (1) select the form for recording, (2) set a specific time for recording the "I know—I think—I will try or do" statement, (3) develop a plan for final analysis and self-evaluation.

VIII. Student Journal

The student, either through oral or written entries develops an accumulated document that reflects his or her reactions to specific learning. The student must (1) select the form of entry, (2) set type of entry examples, (a) specific knowledge gained, (b) application of a knowledge, (c) open end,

(3) set standards for entry, (4) specify time of entry, (5) determine final self-evaluation plan.

Unit:
Dates of Implementation:

Areas of subject integration when unit is thematic:
_____ physical education
_____ language arts
_____ science
_____ math
_____ social studies
_____ art
_____ music

Teacher defined basic outcomes:
   Academic

   Social

Areas for student selection of in-depth investigations (student selects one):

Outline and time frame of teacher directed activities:

Assigned reading/time line:

Teacher led direct teach areas:
   Designate lecture, class involvement, specific group integration, open meeting, motivational meeting, process meeting, basic task group, cooperative task group, base group

Audio visual presentation

Special speakers, guests

Figure 7.   Model for Student Self-Assessment

Name: **Date:**
Area of in-depth study:
Statements of anticipated outcomes (what I want to learn):

Select product that demonstrates learned outcomes
_____ written report
_____ oral presentation
_____ visual presentation
            _____ diagram
            _____ artistic representation
_____ experiment
_____ video presentation
_____ facilitation of class discussion

Plan of investigation (select areas for your investigation—keep notes, information from even areas of ink types)

Reading options—type, amount, time line
_____ magazines   _____ textbooks
_____ notes   _____ encyclopedias
_____ newspapers   _____ books—fiction

Interviews
_____ expert in subject   _____ parent
_____ peers   _____ brother/sister
_____ teacher or in-school person   _____ neighbor

View specific television shows

Experiments

Pertinent information from teacher directed activities

Benchmark to ensure quality
Sources to provide feedback as the product is continually developing to higher quality. (Specify when and how the sources are to be used.)

Possible benchmark sources: parents, teacher, peers, expert

Source
Who:
When:
What feedback do you want?

Presentation of quality product

Analysis of self-assessment

    Amount and quality of work involved

    Analysis of finished product

    Amount of knowledge gained

    Neatness of product

    Success of presentation of finished product

    Assigned grade ___ or percentage ___ when designated

Figure 8.   Student Designed Learning Action Plan

5

Developing a
Noncoercive Classroom

Fear takes a horrible toll. Fear is all around, robbing people of their pride, hurting them, robbing them of a chance to contribute. It is unbelievable what happens when you eliminate fear. (Walton, p. 72)

How do we manage the classroom without the use of rewards and fear? In order to do this we must first realize that rewards and fear are an integral part of traditional classroom management. It is considered the motivational force in our prevalent style of management.

The idea behind the manipulation of reward and punishment management is that we can make others do what we believe they should do. We can make students learn, make them socially responsible, make them happy, make them like school and be "active" participants. With this as the accepted assumption, why is management by reward and punishment so destructive? How does it detract from and undermine quality? These questions will be the focus of this chapter.

Most young children come to school eager to learn and wanting to please the teacher. They are at varying levels of social skill development, yet they all want the teacher's attention and they desire to be successful little people.

Most kindergartens are highly productive places, especially once the trauma of separation from home has subsided. When I was an elementary principal, one of the real pleasures of the job was to spend time, early in the school year, in the kindergarten classes. The enthusiasm for learning, the willingness to join in (sometimes too much willingness), the beginning development of social skills, the varying creative activities for them to join and the noise and movement made the classroom a very need satisfying place.

Seldom did I see teacher behavior that was threatening the student by the use of power and fear, nor was there much evidence of external rewards. Occasionally, I would see a sticker on a student's paper and once in a while a student would be isolated, put into time out. As the school year progressed, and during the long haul after Christmas break, many significant changes started to take place.

More requirements were being placed on the student, requirements which caused them to spend more time at directed academic works with specific expectations on levels of accomplishment and less time on experimenting with learning—in short: requirements which announced the expectation to settle down and get to work. With these changes came more use of stickers and graphs of work accomplished, more controlled teacher use of verbal and non-verbal responses and cues to get the wanted response, and more use of scolding and time out. It worked: the little people wanted the approval of the teacher and they responded in a controlled manner.

I made it a practice to be part of the ending of their day by being present and having them share about their day. The students that had worked for the rewards and had papers with stars on them, stickers for good behavior, and happy smiles always wanted to share their accomplishments with me. Not realizing what I was doing, I would compliment them, and then look at all the faces that had no rewards. I was sending the message, "You can get my approval, too. All you have to do is work hard and get these stickers." I didn't realize at that time that we were already programming the winners and those who would definitely be the losers.

We can't say reward/punishment management doesn't work, because it does, as long as the recipient wants approval or is afraid of the person granting the reward or handing out the punishment. Most young school age children, from kindergarten through third grade, accept and respond to the system because they want a close personal relationship with the teacher. The winners get more self confidence and more rewards, thus becoming more skilled at knowing how to please, how to produce more work, and how to become more proficient at academic skills. They keep climbing. They are becoming the winners in the system. They keep on trying. Teachers know how to give them just enough rewards, with the fear of rejection, to keep them at the job of being "hard working" students.

The process of coercive management, "I'm going to make you do what I want you to do, by the manipulation of rewards and punishment," continues to work with the majority of the young students who find academic success relatively easy. Their self perception of being good successful learners and receiving recognition in the process by reward management opens the possibility for them to become the involved students throughout their school careers. With their belonging need being met by the teacher, the power need being met by being above average achievers, they continue to gain self confidence during middle school. They then become the participants in the extra curricular activities. They are the joiners and those who succeed in the extra curricular areas of music, art, drama, sports, and special academic programs. They continue their involvement in all areas of school programs for the publicity and recognition it provides.

When I ask high school teachers how many hard working quality work producers they have in each of their classes, they say that there are four or five. From this feedback I would estimate that the reward system is effective, at least to the point of getting students to do the work, for about twenty percent of the students. I refer to the reward system of management when referring to the top achievers, as they are seldom subjected to punish management. When I talk to them, I find that hardly ever have they been expelled from school, been truant, spent time in time out areas within the classroom, sent to the principal's office, had their parents called to school due to a problem or experienced any of the other management principles that relate to punishment.

I then ask the teachers about the working habits and production of the rest of the class members. They say about fifteen or approximately two-thirds of the class are not concerned with high quality work and do just enough to get by. They aren't problem makers, they came to class, but show little motivation or interest in what is being taught, and produce minimal work.

This middle group, which comprises the majority of the student body, stopped the process of having high quality, high production work some time during their schooling. When they start kindergarten, they all show a desire to be high producers, high quality workers.

I believe they discontinue their perception of quality when they begin to meet hard work that has a lower frequency of success. They have been conditioned by reward management to expect praise or material reward for achievement, socially, and academically. When they start not meeting a high frequency of rewards, they stop working, their achievement lessens, and the rewards become fewer and farther apart. As the students receive less recognition from the teacher, they learn to anticipate less and the need for teacher approval becomes less of a need. Once the need for approval no longer exists, the idea of working hard for rewards no longer exists. At this point, the students develop strategies to "just get by" and high quality work is no longer a consideration. This is the beginning of the work ethic that creates mediocre to inferior products.

The approximate sixty percent of the students that make up this group experience school with minimal reward or fear management. They come to class, do enough work to get by, aren't discipline problems, are minimally involved in class discussions, minimally involved in school activities, and get by. The idea of "just enough to get by" is the attitude they take from school.

One of the real losses from coercive management comes when we realize and acknowledge the fact that we have a non-involved citizenry and a society that accepts indifference as the norm. This attitude of indifference is learned.

A second tragedy of coercive, reward/punishment management is that sixty percent of the students do not realize their own potential. As the system becomes indifferent to them, they stop the challenge for excellence and perceive themselves as average or below average. Once they have their perception reinforced by teachers, they develop work standards that justify their perception and accept average to below average work.

For approximately twenty percent of the students, reward/punishment management becomes totally ineffective. For these students, the rigors of behavioral and academic expectations placed upon them simply become too much. Due to inherent and learned limitations, they are incapable of producing work and behavior that is acceptable of rewards when compared to same-aged peers.

The regular education classroom teachers, as they manage by rewarding good behavior for academic achievement and behavior have minimal opportunity to respond to these students with rewards. These students take an exorbitant amount of time and energy and, as the rest of the class progresses, their accomplishments are minimal. The use of fear management is then instituted to force them to comply and they become more unmanageable. The teacher then is at a loss for alternatives and the feelings of frustration and hopelessness follow. This is followed by a need to justify non-effectiveness and the student is referred for intellectual or psychological evaluation. The problem is placed in the student. Ten percent of these students are then separated from their manageable peers and are programmed in alternate schools or exceptional education, the other ten percent struggle and continue to fail in the classroom. They produce no high quality work, and fear management becomes the norm.

I had better define, at this point, what is meant by reward/punishment management. Reward management is incentive management. The idea is that students will work hard to receive a reward, and through the distribution of the rewards quality work will be accomplished. Teachers have an incredible number of these incentives built into their management repertoire: words, smiles, nods, stories, grades, stickers, charts—the list goes on. We normally deliver these incentives after we have done an informal or formal inspection, so the students are conditioned to watch and wait for the approval. This, in turn, grants us almost total control over the classroom!

Punish management infers that we will implement a consequence to an act that will cause the student displeasure. We seldom induce direct physical pain such as hitting, but instead we use withdrawal of pleasure and/or psychological control. The most common type of punish management is threatening behavior. The message is: "You had better get your work done or you will miss recess; or you will fail the test," etc. Teachers impose the factor of fear, fear that something bad will happen unless students do what they're supposed to do.

Examples of fear management are pink slips, detentions, name on the board, missed recess, exclusion from non-curricular events, etc. Coupled with the threatening behavior comes the skill of using rejection of approval. This is the "ignore it and it will go away" phenomenon, the serious disapproval look, the physical separation of the student from peers, the special time out area where there is no visual contact with the rest of the students, and this list also goes on.

I observed the set consequence coercive management style at work in a third grade classroom. One of the agreed upon rules was that no one was to interrupt when another person was talking. The consequence for interruption was semi-isolation in an in-classroom time out area. It was at the beginning of the school year and schedules were still being set, so there was much confusion and changes of schedules happening. The teacher was attempting to set a model of being in control and enforcing the rules and consequences. A student realized he was supposed to be released from class to meet with his Chapter I teacher. I could see his level of discomfort as he realized if he interrupted the teacher he would be in trouble, and if he was late for the specialist he would be in trouble. He was fidgeting and off task. He finally took control and spoke out that he was supposed to leave and go to Chapter I, only to have his behavior related to the set rule of not interrupting. He was then sent to the time out area to think about what he had done so a plan could be made to not allow it to happen again. I watched him in the time out area. He was now feeling great frustration for missing the specialist and being in trouble as well as being used as an example of how discipline was being established. He sat as though he couldn't believe what was happening to him, with no power to change it.

The coercive management system worked, to some degree, when we were a society that was built around semi-isolation. The family was the primary center of communication and value development and the school fostered and projected the same values. One of the values that was expounded was that the title parent or teacher granted the adult authority, respect, and power. The home and school became the two primary teaching institutions, and projected this value. The majority of the students spent up to eight years or so in school, then left to do physical labor, often times staying within a close proximity of their original home.

Those days are gone, replaced by the influence of television, sophisticated advertising and affluence. With these influences came changes in values. One of the changes that directly affects teaching and parenting is that the title of authority alone no longer insures respect or power. Respect and the power of the title have to be earned, and when the adult will not accept the challenge young people rebel.

For most young people, the first major psychological rebellion leading to the start of separation from adults occurs around eleven. This separation is demonstrated by wanting more time alone and less time talking to or being with adults. This is the transitional period, the beginnings of separation from those who hold authority over them. Along with the separation comes more moodiness, more listening to their music, more television, and alone time as they search for forms of independence and identity. Physical changes begin that are confusing, embarrassing, and which often place them in awkward positions when relating to their peers (especially the opposite sex). This is a time of dynamic and intense change in the pre-teen's life and life-style.

The pre-adolescent's need to please adults is replaced by the gang age and the need for belonging and approval quickly changes to need of peer approval. As the changes intensify, adults increase the manipulation of rewards and punishments in an attempt to coerce them into behaving and learning, only now they no longer respond as they did when they were primary age students.

Reward/punishment management now becomes the main source for their justification for separation, as they make the adjustment from adult to peer approval. The system turns on itself as the students gain the knowledge of how to use the coercive system against their teachers and parents. They gain in peer approval when they openly defy adults, project an image of apathy, and produce inferior quality work.

The sixty percent of the students that were struggling to be winners has stopped the struggle and quality work no longer exists.

Students are somewhat connected to school during this period of time. It's the place where they meet their friends, have some involvement in extra curricular areas, do some work, and get by.

The second major change period starts around sixteen and leads to a more complete sense of separation. A large portion of the students in the sixty percent majority begin to realize their independence. They become the workers in the minimal paying job market. Grocery stores, fast food chains, car wash operations, and numerous other businesses hire the young workers. This gives the students their first taste of financial independence and a powerful sense of control over their lives. A second factor contributing to their lives is the ownership of a driver's license. This further opens up the sense of independence through the freedom of mobility, again freeing them from adult dependency. The third significant factor is that they begin to break away from their strong peer involvement and begin to relate to a person of the opposite sex. This is when their first real sense of a reciprocally caring relationship with someone who is not part of their family becomes a reality.

For many, the need for adult dependency is now over, and adults, namely parents and teachers, are lost as to how to respond. There is a tendency for them to try to get tough at this point. More punishment management than what was normally used is now attempted. The result is greater separation because the person who is punishing is no longer need fulfilling to the teen. The teacher or parent, as well as the punishment itself, is rejected by the young person.

High school teachers talk about the non-motivated students and they try to develop strategies to get them going; to do the work that the school says is important. When I talk with teachers about these students, they relate that working with them is the most difficult aspect of teaching. As these students continually emulate the message that school isn't important, and what is important is their world outside of school. Some states have gone to the point of passing coercive legislation in an attempt to curb work outside school, assuming that work will improve in school if outside involvement is curtailed.

It won't improve, as a new world of work, fun, and relationships has replaced school.

It is difficult for the high school teacher to stay enthusiastic and motivated to teach. The top twenty percent that now dominates school activities and continues to work hard become the source of inspiration. It's those few good students and the associated classes that give meaning to a day of teaching.

For the sixty percent that has separated from the need of teacher approval and has invested its interest outside of school, high school becomes a holding tank, with minimal quality and non-productive learning the norm. For the ten percent that aren't in exceptional education but see school as a place not to be, we create laws with negative consequences that make them go to school and learn. The system continues to fail.

Those that have perfected the skill to do minimal to inferior quality work are the work force that the schools send out to become workers in our industrial plants, technicians in service areas, workers in construction, receptionists in offices, para-professionals in the health related businesses, sales people in stores, maintenance workers, etc. We continue to hear the plea from the business community to develop better work ethics and quality workers. They want workers who are interested in their jobs and want to do quality work; workers who know how to cooperate and relate to others. Our present management system isn't working. Eight out of twelve school years of the attitude that "as long as I can get by—it's good enough" has taken its toll in later work production—in work quality ethics. The attitude ingrained in the school system (non quality expectations) passes on to the job market, creating poor quality workers, poor quality products, and poor management skills. Attempting to get students to work by reward or punishment management, pushing them psychologically with the boss management technique of "do it or else" or even giving the all too common message that "it's o.k. to be non-productive while in my class as long as you don't bother anyone else" has its consequences: consequence with strong repercussions.

MANAGING THE CLASS IN A NONCOERCIVE MANNER

For a classroom teacher, it becomes next to impossible to change the system. We do have the power to change the classroom, and perhaps as this happens the student will also be free to change. To move a classroom from one that is coercively managed to one that uses noncoercion will not be an easy transition.

Reward management will always be part of classroom management. But, the emphasis in a quality classroom that is noncoercive will change it from being highly dependent upon teacher approval to highly dependent upon individual student approval. Chapter 2, getting the student in touch with quality, Chapter 3, providing the necessary connections for the student to sense quality relationships, and Chapter 4, moving from a model of inspection to self assessment all address the issue of assisting the student to become self motivated toward quality work.

The student will need to continue to receive teacher approval, and as the one who is more in control of their own learning, will seek assistance and incorporate teacher suggestion into the learning products. It is very different when the students ask for help than when they are manipulated by rewards, or told to do something or they will suffer a negative consequence. Quality management demands that the student continually learn the skills of self management. Quality management dictates that our job is to get students to understand relationships and develop the skills of self motivation, self choice of products, and self assessment to help them sense the strong personal satisfaction that comes from creating quality products.

Establish an Understanding of Partnershipping

The first step of quality management requires establishment of a classroom understanding. The understanding is one of partnership—"We're in this together." I want to be a successful teacher and have a right to be one. You want to be a successful student and you have the right to be one. What do we need to do so these two rights can be realized? The school year begins with discussion and negotiations of these two rights, which leads to a working definition. As long as the working definition of successful teacher and successful student is working, quality work can prevail. If the teacher's right to teach and the student's right to learn breaks down, redefinition is necessary. New discussion and negotiation must be opened. Thus, a continuous process spans the year. Negotiation replaces coercion as the environment for creating partnershipping is created.

Students respond to the idea of partnershipping. I study and watch what teachers do who have the skills to develop partnerships with their learners. The sense that everyone is in control of their own areas of responsibility is the first indicator. There aren't charts on the wall reminding students what they are to do and how well they have done. Nor are assignments written and kept on the board to remind students what they are to be working on.

Some student learning spaces are neat and tidy while others have a degree of clutter indicating individual choice and showing teacher/student partnership based on respect.

I am continually amazed at how ingenious, responsible and positive students respond when they are allowed to take control of their own immediate space and create systems for reminding themselves of their responsibilities. We must learn how to assist, then trust students to take responsibility instead of the more prevalent coercive management style of attempting to force responsibility.

Continuous Definition of Responsibility

The second significant structure of noncoercive management is the need to define (between teacher and student) who is responsible for what. This definition of responsibility takes place at both the whole-class discussion and at the individual student level. When a student begins his/her project, there should be no confusion about what each party has agreed to do.

At the beginning of a unit of study, be it a major unit that will last over a period of time or a daily lesson, the shared responsibilities between teacher and students must be stated and understood. In the partnership agreement the teacher might agree to provide a common base of knowledge by direct teaching, provide some specific reading material, and agree to be available for individual consultation. The teacher might facilitate a class discussion at the completion of the unit or lesson.

The students might agree to take some notes during the direct teach portion of the lesson. They could decide if they would use the provided reading material or find their own. They could make a decision if they want to work individually or in pairs, and choose optional ways of preparing for class discussion. They might take written notes to refer to or "wing it" as they prepare a learning product.

The projects could be skits, rap songs, oral reports, visual reports, or whatever. The point here is that they have creative freedom to choose and develop their learning project.

They then decide if the project is going to have self assessment or a combination of self assessment with teacher assessment. Now everyone is ready to go to work! Students need this type of detailed understanding. Once they have it, they can begin to do a quality job.

In a teacher directed coercively managed class, there is often ten minutes of students questioning for clarification of assignments and their attempts to redefine the work to be of a lesser amount. The teacher assumes major responsibility for the students' learning and spends considerable time in preparation of direct teaching, having all materials ready for the learners, grading, and recording. This results in the mind set and procedure that "this is what you are to do, this is how you will do it, this is what is required, and this is what you will learn."

I've watched teachers who have perfected partnership agreement strategies and the process is not time consuming. As in the coercive managed classroom it requires about ten minutes of discussion to start work as shared responsibility. The students take on added, agreed upon responsibility for their learning and empowers self to take control. Students buy into work when they have the power to choose what they are to do, how they will do it, and thoroughly understand the entire process.

Classroom Rules

The third point of noncoercive management centers on the establishment and implementation of classroom rules. Agreed upon rules regarding behavior and work ethics are a necessary structure in all classrooms. All rules are established for the same basic reasons—they guarantee rights and establish security. These rights are the rights of teachers to teach, rights of students to learn, rights of dignity, and rights of not having someone misuse power and cause fear.

Pre-determined consequences for the breaking of rules in an "in control" coercive environment allows no flexibility for enforcement and destroys the option for discussion, understanding, negotiating, and learning new more effective ways to behave. The coercive managed classroom with set consequences eliminates the possibility for flexible interpretation and the opportunity to personalize, based upon individual student differences. This process eliminates negotiation and partnershipping and destroys the basis of noncoercive management.

Rules become the source of power struggles between teachers and students when the students are not rule oriented. Once the rule has been stated, they now have the mechanism by which to rebel against the rule and its enforcer—the teacher.

The teacher, due to the prevalent management system of reward/punishment, has the self expectation that being in control means they must interpret rules as being the same for all students. The principle expectancy placed upon teachers to have an orderly classroom again plays into the system. When one reviews the process that is used to get a student in line—a student who is choosing to break the rules—the process is to punish bad behavior, reward good behavior. This is accomplished through pre-set consequences which are always implemented the same way, ignoring individual differences and unique circumstances.

One of the greatest fallacies of classroom management is the notion that if we ignore rule breaking, it will go away. The reasons for breaking them are either to see how far the limit can be pushed or to define a basis for the struggle for power. Ignore the behavior and the limit is pushed farther. Respond to the behavior by engaging the consequences and the beginning of "who will win?" struggle is implemented. When we attempt to find good behavior and reward it, the students have defined their playing rules differently. They are engineering the encounter to center around the breaking of rules, not playing by them. In the majority of our classrooms, there is a student who is getting an exorbitant amount of teacher time and energy, with very minimal success because of the choice to break the rules.

Noncoercive Rule Management

The noncoercive classroom management system will continue to have rules, but will change in two significant ways. The first is that there must be a continual emphasis behind the reason for the rules. It isn't enough to just get class agreement on rules at the beginning of the school year, post them in the room, and proceed with follow up enforcement. Students must continually understand how rules benefit them, what they get personally by accepting and following reasonable rules, and how their class will profit by having rules. It needs to be emphasized as whole class lessons, in every day circumstances, as a school-wide awareness program, and through involvement of the school community. The second major change regarding rules revolves around negotiation and non-negotiation, which take place between the teacher and the student regarding enforcement for following the rules. The rules are developed and understood in the context of being either negotiable or non-negotiable. This understanding opens the way for individual teacher student discussion and the individuality of enforcement.

One of the real drawbacks of being able to work individually with who that are breaking rules, and becoming behavior problems in the reward/punishment model, is the issue of fairness. The coercive management style is built upon the premise that everyone has to be treated the same, regardless of circumstance, and once a rule is established, it must consistently be followed through for all. Yet, we know that in a classroom, there has to be continual adjustment for student needs, learning abilities, social development, living circumstances, and attitudes about following rules. This is a factor that makes classroom management difficult management—there is the need to continually reassess and adjust for differences. We do a reasonably good job of readjustment in most areas, but rule enforcement is not one of them. We then set the stage for difficulty in the most complex aspect of classroom management—behavior management. The noncoercive classroom has, at its core, a central message: "In this room we will sit down, individually talk things out, and reach a reasonable understanding that you and I can respect and abide by."

One of my grandchildren just started his kindergarten year. He is a bus rider and, being an afternoon student, begins his day riding without all the big kids. He came home from school the other day and informed his mother that he would like to break one of the school bus rules. She asked him just what rule it was, and he explained that all the kids are supposed to look straight ahead (and into the back of the head of the student in front of them). Willy thought this was very unreasonable because he greatly enjoyed looking out the window. After some discussion, Willy and his mother decided that it was okay to break this rule as long as he didn't disturb other students. Was this rule necessary in the first place? I can't say for sure, but certainly a student's right to look out the school bus window should, at the very least, be respected, and the rule open to compromise and negotiation.

Non-Negotiable Rules

In all classrooms there are some behaviors that cannot be accepted under any circumstance. These behaviors center on using physical force to hurt a person or verbally attacking another to purposely destroy their dignity. These behaviors are non-negotiable and result in the implementation of immediate understood consequences. The consequence is then carried to its defined limit and discussion of how to behave in a more responsible manner is discussed at a later time.

Negotiable Rules

The majority of classroom rules pertain to basic principles of how to cooperate, respect others and self, and implement work habits. They are the rules that negotiation happens and constitute the majority that pertain to classroom management. Most of these pertain to insuring an orderly working environment and refer to such things as quietness, promptness, neatness, work handed in on time, etc. These rules must have the opportunity for negotiation to insure flexibility, right to be discussed, be personalized, and altered to meet individual circumstances. There are no pre-set consequences. They are written in general statements and are designed to promote discussion, to build understandings, and to teach strategies of how to be more responsible. The right to negotiate is basic to their purpose.

The rule is not what is negotiated. The discussion between the student and teacher centers on why the rule is important, what caused the disregard for the rule, a plan to do something different so the rule will not be broken in the future, and an agreed upon consequence if it is broken. There is no upset on either the student's or teacher's behalf, no anger or high emotion, just the continued message that we will work this problem out so you can feel OK about the solution, and so can I.

In the noncoercive classroom, this purpose is respected. The student and teacher sit down and talk the situation out, reach understandings, and personalize plans of how to become more responsible when the same circumstances are again present. It is in the discussion and personalizing of the plan that new and more responsible ways of behaving are taught.

In the reward/punishment, pre-determined consequence classroom, the right to negotiate is seldom allowed—in fact, if the student attempts to explain, it is often seen as an attempt at trying to get out of work, as a defiance to get what he/she wants, or as someone who is spoiled at home and gets whatever they want, and the perceptions go on. The teacher is unable to discuss with the students as the consequence is immediate and set into motion. The student may have justifiable reasons for his/her behavior but is denied the opportunity to discuss and learn new behavior.

Shared Decision Making

Shared decision making evolves as a natural outcome of noncoercive management and is built upon the right to negotiate. Shared decisions take place when there is a willingness to share power, and they become commonplace in noncoercive management. This sharing of power is one of the prime factors in increased work productivity and gaining a higher quality of work produced. When students have a say in what they will do and how they will do it, they become committed to quality.

I was sharing with a first grade teacher who was in the transitional process of moving from coercive to noncoercive management, and she stated how she had, in the past, underestimated the work abilities and the sense of personal responsibility students had. I asked her what was allowing her to see greater potential in her students now. She responded that as she retrained herself to feel less responsible for all that happened in the classroom and gave greater authority to the first graders for their own learning and sense of self control, the more responsible they became. The more she was able to give up the idea of needing to be in charge, the more positive and willing the students became to take on responsibilities. She said that the high levels of quality being created by the students were directly related to their ability to be decision makers.

Breaking Down the Barriers—Shared Decision Making

Shared decision making has the built in components of trust and confidence with both parties. Coercive management destroys these two important factors as it drives itself from the perspective of superior to inferior. I am the teacher, you are the student. I am the superior, you are the inferior. I am the principal, you are the teacher. I am superior, you are inferior. Shared decision making cannot happen until these barriers are broken down.

By definition, teacher has more power than student, principal has more power than teacher, superintendent has more power than principal. Our system of decision making in schools works on this higher echelon system. It is not easy to break down the barriers that prevent trust and confidence of shared decision making. However, breaking down these often hidden barriers of control and power is the necessary element of making quality a reality.

A principal was recently discussing her attempt to have shared decision making as the way she and the faculty worked together. She talked about how hard it was to get redefinition of who was responsible for what decisions and the reluctance of the staff to take on areas of decision making that had traditionally been administrative responsibilities. During the conversation she stated that the staff was becoming involved in the decision to purchase major equipment for the school and then asked if I thought she should grant them the right to have access to the funds and the decision to spend the money as they thought it should be spent. I understood why they were having difficulty with shared decision making as the withholding of funds was central to the issue of who held the power.

Shared decision making with students often falls into the same dilemma. We work out the plan together but in the final stages of the agreement I will hold the power as I'm not sure I can trust you to do what you say you will. The confidence for future shared decisions then becomes blocked as the student quickly learns "I'm not a competent decision maker and, in the end, it will be the teacher's decision anyway."

I realize the movement from coercive management to noncoercive management in the classroom is a major shift. In our training as teachers, the minimal amount of classroom management instruction we receive is centered around coercive management techniques such as enforcement schedules, sharing and recording student progress, and developing lesson plans. This implies that we set the course of study and develop learning strategies for the students, evaluate and grade, and use assertive discipline strategies—all indicating we are to be in total control. We often find ourselves in a work place that has the expectation that we are to be in charge of our classroom. This is interpreted as having and exerting control over our students. We go into large classes, relying on what we have been trained to do—coercive management. It's much easier (and faster) to impose a consequence than to sit down and work out a noncoercive, negotiated plan.

The problem with coercive management is what it does to the classroom over an extended period. Coercive manipulating, through reward reinforcement results in the students doing "just enough" to get rewarded. Using fear sets in place the development of behaviors that attempt to avoid the pain. The system provides the student with an opportunity to develop strategies for minimal work and avoidance, which results in inferior work habits and minimal self responsibility.

Noncoercive management changes the classroom atmosphere to one of being involved in the decisions of learning and working. It establishes a partnership agreement, continually defines responsibility and shared decision making, and uses rules as a source for learning.

COMMUNICATION MODEL

Respect of individual dignity is basic to noncoercive management. The communication model that is used has to reflect this belief. Anger, ridicule, sarcasm, and an air of superiority are all based upon wanting to control degrading individual dignity and have no place in quality classroom management.

Understanding the how and whys of what drives human behavior is fundamental to developing a noncoercive communication model. The communication and behavior model that will be explained is based upon a model developed by Dr. William Glasser, called Reality Therapy and Control Theory. It is explained by my interpretation and application of the model through the experiences I have had as an educator and psychologist.

The first understanding, when communicating with a student, is to understand the forces that drive the choice making. The forces are always the same, even if the person is shouting and angry, quiet and listening, or talking and agreeing. They believe that whatever behavior they are engaging in will result in their eventually getting what they want and will minimize pain and maximize control. These two forces are basic to why anyone makes the choices they do. There are continual choices made to balance the two. The student may choose to maximize pain in the attempt to maximize control, or will give up control to minimize pain, but the two factors are always present in choice making.

I watched a high school junior, while in the assistant principal's office, agonize over the balance. He had been expelled from a classroom for calling a teacher a "prick" after they had engaged in an argument over a cap he was wearing. He entered the office still displaying the anger and using it in an attempt to maintain control. The assistant principal was able to relate to him and through discussion his anger subsided, and they were then able to analyze the long term effects of the behavior and he realized the potential of increased pain if his parents became involved. The assistant principal then left to talk to the teacher and returned saying the teacher wanted an apology and then he could return to class, which would cause him to have to give up control. Two variables were now exposed, increased pain or loss of control. There was no way he could accomplish the balance of minimizing pain and maximizing control.

The second understanding is that in order for each individual student to maintain the balance they must be able to open four success pathways; fun, freedom, belonging, and power. When the student has the ways and means to open the pathways it is normally easy to communicate with them as they are future oriented, producing work, compatible, and making choices that balance the minimal pain and maximal control phenomena. They have temporary setbacks as one or two of the pathways close for a while, and they become frustrated or disillusioned. They have experienced enough success in their life and have developed a repertoire of alternative ways to reopen the pathways, and are reasonable and willing to communicate in a way that will give them the control to reopen their pathways. They may argue a bit, or close down and become noncommunicative, but the anger, disappointment, or withdrawal is temporary and is replaced with choices that move them forward.

It is imperative that quality classroom managers know their students well enough to know if they have the success pathways open, as it is basic to how they are communicated with.

The third understanding is to realize and be able to identify the student that has the pathways closed. These students live in a world of continual self perceiving pain and loss of control. Depending upon the self perceived degree of pain and loss of control, it becomes paramount in their choice making behavior, and directly reflects upon building positive communication patterns. The student who has open pathways engage in behaviors that cause them to be futuristic in their thinking and expanding their choices, resulting in continually developing more and more options to balance pain and control. The student that has or perceives to have the pathways closed also engaged in thinking but it becomes present or past oriented and they begin a psychological journey, attempting to find the way to not hurt and gain control. They enter into funneling their choice making continually closing down options and alternatives, as they progress in their attempt to find the option that stops the pain and offers control. The pain results from a number of sources, such as self or significant others not being able to meet expectations, rejection, loneliness, continual failures, physical or psychological abuse, and physical or mental inadequacies. As the pain intensifies, the sense of loss of control intensifies, and the journey intensifies.

The first stage in the process results in a series of behaviors that are built upon denial. The thinking is based upon a central idea, if I can develop a rationale that what is expected of me is of no value to who I am or what I am expected to do, I can reject the expectation. The process of giving up and not trying makes and acts upon a giving up choice, they sense less pain than attempting to continue to work out and not be successful and a significant sense of immediate control. For most students, this giving up behavior begins with the giving up of academic accomplishments. They don't finish their work on time, attempt to hand in assignments that are partially done, distract the lesson by talking or bothering others, not have their materials ready to do work, argue about the amount of work, etc. The quality of their work is in a continual downslide.

The younger learner needs communication at this time that helps them assess their ability to be a successful worker, to explore their values about the work, expected to delve into areas where they have skills, and easy expectations in the deficit area. This seldom happens and instead, the learner finds more emphasis on his/her deficit area, with additional work expected, resulting in greater frustration and pain and sense of loss of control. They then move to the second stage of funneling.

At the second stage, they discontinue the denial and accept the fact that they are unable to compete. They then fully realize the pain and loss of control that results from inadequacies, and they attempt to discover the cause of the problem. They no longer try to successfully complete academic work as that phase of attempting to gain control is past. They now center on relationships to find their cause of the problem. They transfer their thinking from academic expectations to people expectations, as they have already removed academic performance to a place of minimal to no value.

During this stage of funneling, they exert considerable energy in their attempt to find the cause of the problem, as they believe they can regain control and relieve the pain by knowing how to focus to cause change. As they explore the people aspect, they develop a thinking pattern that emphasizes a me or they understanding. Either they, those people and their expectations that are attempting to control my world are the cause of my pain, or the cause is me. It's my own fault due to my own self held perceived inadequacies.

The students gravitate between the two perspectives and they operationalize a behavior style that has a they or me base of understanding. At times they are aggressive as they attempt to control the people and experiences that they believe are causing them that pain and loss of control. They verbally attack peers and adults, become defiant when asked to cooperate or produce work and employ argumentative communication. If their verbal aggressiveness isn't effective, then physical aggression can follow. They are attempting to control those that they believe are controlling them.

When the controller gains control by position, fear or rewards, direct results of the control cause the controlled to sense a loss of control. The controlled then stops aggressing and turns inward to rationalize the pain and loss of control. In order to psychologically survive, the person then removes the controller from their real world and attempts to gain control by building a wall around self as an insulation from the pain. The inward journey has numerous possibilities: depression, psychosomatic illness, creating voices that talk to them, and suicide. Each of the possibilities gives the person a sense of control and a reduction of pain, and for some it becomes their source of survival.

As students make choices during this stage of the funnel, their behavior can become extremely erratic and one day be highly aggressive followed by withdrawal and nonparticipation. It is during the time of withdrawal that they may remove the teacher psychologically from their world and then, during a period of aggression, become violent and attack.

Some students that are funneling their choices at stage two reach a conclusion that one of the two behavior styles gives them minimal pain and maximal control. They then adapt that style and use it when other crises appear.

This one behavior style to deal with crisis is the third stage of the funnel. They have experimented with a variety of choices and behavior styles and have reached the conclusion that either aggression or withdrawal gives them the balance. They now have reduced their alternatives to a single plan and, for some of them, it will become their way to cope forever.

For some students that are in the funnel, starting in middle school or high school, they realize that there is a quick and easy way to minimize pain and gain a sense of control. Drugs become readily available to them and as they experiment they discover that the effects of the drug give them a sense of the balance they are seeking. They quickly move to the fourth stage of the funnel, addiction. They have now reduced their alternatives to one choice and as crises erupt, they use.

As we develop a communication model with students we must understand how different it is to communicate with students that have the success pathways open versus those that don't. In both cases, the students have the same self perception which is one of being successful. The major difference is one is expanding, exploring, and including where the other is narrowing and excluding. The more either are able to fulfill their self perception, the more successful they perceive themselves to be. The students funneling their choices do so by continually creating crises which allows them to employ their controlling strategies.

The aggressive student becomes highly skilled at manipulation and emotionalization and attempts to cause the communication to become coercive.

When their goal is accomplished, they reaffirm their perception that the problem is outside of them as the person who is attempting to communicate doesn't like them or is trying to force them to do something.

The student that withdraws avoids all interaction by not being involved verbally or nonverbally. They seldom cause any problems and, if capable, will do the expected work. When asked to participate in class discussion, they do the minimum and display no interest in what is being taught or how teaching is being done. The reaction to their behavior is not to include them which fulfills their perception of what they want.

Noncoercive communication must guarantee the communicator to be able to express his/her self and not be drawn into a role that is designed by the receiver of the communication. This is not an easy task as the achievers are continually trying to find out what the teacher wants so they can give back the right answers and the students that are funneling are trying to promote a coercive emotional response.

The model has to be built upon knowing each student as an individual and responding to their individuality. This requires that the teacher is involved at a personal level and knows the student other than his/her academic achievement. It is during the building of a relationship based upon the student's nonacademic world where the possibility of relating and being accepted by the student is created. The students have to sense a wanting to become involved by the teacher before they begin to consider the possibility. The student controls the possibility for involvement and seldom allows any until they believe that they will not be hurt by the teacher. Students do not allow teachers into their internal worlds when the teacher might increase their pain. Noncoercive communication begins when this trust of caring and wanting to be involved is accepted by the receiver.

Once acceptance is established, the teacher can then begin to discuss sensitive as well as nonsensitive areas. The key is to begin to have the student verbalize about what they are doing. The communication centers on asking the same question, "What are you doing?" in different ways. As the student responds to the questions, they start the process of taking ownership of their behaviors or actions. The teacher stays at a nonemotional level, never expressing anger, criticism, revenge, or placing their own values into the student's world. There is no change of behavior until the student accepts ownership of the behavior.

The ownership of behavior is followed by helping the student develop valuing understandings about the behavior. They are asked to think about and discuss the behavior in terms of "Is it getting you what you want?" The discussion helps the student identify what they want and then make a value judgment regarding the behavior to determine if it is helping them get what they want. It is in the relationship of assessing the behavior and making value judgments that causes behavioral change. If the student reaches the conclusion that what they are doing isn't helping them get what they want, then a logical step is to ask them if they want to make a plan that will get them what they want. Most students express a wanting to make the plan as they have chosen to begin a new way.

If the student assesses the behavior and determines it is getting him what he wants, but is distracting others from getting what they want, then an open honest dialog must continue. The teacher, stating his/her case unemotionally, explains that he/she can't be an effective teacher or students can't be effective learners if the behavior continues and consequences are laid out and agreed upon by the student. If the behavior is one that does not effect others, such as completing assigned work or doing the daily lessons, then it is explained that he/she will fall behind the other students and continuing consequences will follow the nonwork attitude. The student is then given the freedom of choice to complete work or not.

It is important that the student understand and agree to the consequence of nonproductive behavior that is keeping others from being productive. They then have taken ownership of the consequences and the system is nonpunitive. If the student decides the nonproductive behavior is getting them what they want, it is assured the behavior will continue, as they are indicating that this values what they are doing. It is the valuing of the behavior that drives the behavior and student change to more responsible behavior must include valuing discussion.

If the student chooses to make a plan for change, then the plan needs to be short, concise, and guarantee success. Try to make the plan nondependent upon others, as the student oftentimes cannot depend upon others to follow through on their part. The plan needs to be self motivating, self rewarding, and primarily designed by the student.

The last part of the model is based upon commitment. At the completion of this plan the teacher assures the student that they are committed to the plan. The commitment is one of assurance that the student is going to be successful, that you are convinced in its possibility of success, and you trust the student to follow through. It is in this commitment that the student gains the confidence and strength to follow through.

If the plan doesn't materialize into a successful attempt, then assure the student that what is needed is a better plan.

6

Time to Do Quality Work

An issue that must be resolved, if quality work is to be the classroom norm, is the teacher's control over time. The three primary sub-issues inherent in this are a balancing of quantity and quality, addressing the continual disturbances which occur throughout the teaching day, and providing the time to work individually or with colleagues for planning.

Quality work requires that the student has time to invest in his/her product. Unfortunately, this idea has been lost as the classroom teacher is required to broaden the scope of what he/she is to teach. It simply is not possible to produce a quality piece of work in a twenty-minute or less segment. Nor is quality produced when the object must continually be interrupted and/or set aside until another time or day. Quality dictates its own time frame and is dependent upon the committed investment of energy over time. This is true whenever quality is to be the outcome, be it in the world of business, or the world of being a student.

Teachers are in a continuous state of conflict over attempts to meet the dictated expectations of state and local educational boards to accomplish all the expectations. The system through overload, creates the feeling of being overwhelmed with all there is to do, and this eventually becomes the feeling of hopelessness.

Quality is forced into mediocrity (at best) as quantity takes priority through dictated curriculum guides and subject expectations. This system of forced curriculum expectations becomes overwhelming as the demand for more subject matter inclusion is required by state departments of public instruction. All specialization areas are represented and continually exert their demands for more time and content. (I believe the only group that is not represented is that of the classroom teacher.) Social studies, health issues, environmental issues, student special needs issues, issues of the arts, national test scores, illiteracy statistics, poverty, and drop out numbers force education into the light of public opinion. The degree of public outrage pertaining to a specific area then becomes the state department's vehicle to demand a solution to the problem. The solution is always the same—add another curriculum or expand an already over-developed one that is already competing for time and priority of importance.

Teachers are forced into inservices for a quickly fixed, patched up resolution to the problem. The classroom teacher must now attempt to include more subject related learning with no additional time allotted. The students then receive a more fragmented school day, as there is never a reduction or elimination of what is already expected. We have reached the point where there is no room to put more in, unless something is taken out.

How does a quality school begin to repair the problem of determining what needs to be taught and reestablish the classroom as a place for quality work? It has to start with the teachers, principal, and parents taking time to set the priorities of the school. The school must decide what it can do and what it can't do within the time constraints of the six or so hours that students are present. These are hard decisions and affect long-held ideas that the school will provide a very diverse program for all the students. There are programs that may need to be moved out of the school day and the school's responsibility, affecting staffing patterns and allowing the school to be used by private enterprise. An example of this is the movement of drivers education from the schools' responsibility and transferring it to private driver training schools. Parts of art, music, and physical education programs may need to have less specialized class time and be replaced with supplementary programs outside the school day. Remedial programs may also be partially serviced outside the school day. The overriding principle is this: if teachers are going to have students do quality work, they must have the time it takes to accomplish quality works.

Two of the most "tinkering" variables (taking the term from Dr. Deming and interpreted as to mean played with but without making significant change) in education are time and grades. Grades, in some manner or another, will always be with us and so will the constraints and frustrations of time. Time is broken up into block/segments in the elementary school for reading, writing, language, sometimes combining the three into a language arts block. Spelling is normally wherever we can find time for it, and the specialists in art, music, physical education, reading, I.M.C., and remedial programs get their times out of the day. The students have recess, noon hour, afternoon breaks, special programs, and in Wisconsin, an occasional snow day. Only teachers can experience the frustration and helplessness of wanting to do quality teaching while students are continually coming into and going out of the classroom. Somewhere we fit in a science lesson, a social studies lesson, and try to find a somewhat set time for math. One of the latest tinkerings is the creation of the six-day school week, staying within the confines of the five day week. Not only are the students confused, but so are most teachers. Obviously, this wasn't designed by teachers.

At the end of a hectic day we're reminded that we forgot to send a student to the nurse, and the music teacher stops to tell us that one of the students was ten minutes late for his violin lesson. Then the principal comes on the public address system and reminds us tomorrow the artist in residence for the week has had to change the time for the all school awards from ten-thirty to one o'clock. That was the only time available for math, and you frantically try to arrange something else so that math won't be missed. . . . and the school year progresses. Time for quality? You must be kidding.

In the present day of cluttered and fragmented curriculum, I believe all students are deprived of a quality experience. This happens because we stay at a surface or beginning level of learning in most areas, particularly in science, social studies, and writing. Yet, these are the areas where individual students can get motivated and want to explore and create in-depth work. When we stop this in-depth exploration the student senses frustration and a loss of control and quickly learns that the best way not to feel this frustration is not to get overly interested in what is being taught.

The process of non-depth exploration starts early in a student's school life. Once the feeling of frustration impacts the mind of the student, it's very difficult to change. My grandson, Willy, after his fourth day in kindergarten, told his mother that he hadn't yet been taught anything new. He had already attended pre-school programs for two years, knew his alphabet and numbers, perceived himself as an artist, and went to kindergarten wanting to continue his artistic perception and learn to read. The homework assignment he brought home was a ditto sheet, numbers one through four, that he was to trace. He can't understand why the paints, easels, brushes, huge sheets of paper, scissors, and glues are all sitting in the art center, and he is tracing numbers. He asked his mom how this was going to help him learn to read and be an artist.

Just as the school needs to sort out what it can and can't do, the classroom teacher's must sort out their beliefs regarding the need for all students having to do all things. Quality classroom management dictates time and commitment, prerequisites for in-depth exploration, prerequisites for producing quality work. All students are not interested in all aspects of what is being taught. They quickly discover areas within the subject matter where they have no desire for in-depth involvement and time invested work. How much of a generalist does a student need to be? Can we excuse them from various lessons, assignments, and units of study, and subject matter to pursue interests?

It is always interesting to investigate the idea of specific in-depth learning vs. generalized learning with teachers, as there is a definite variety of responses. With this idea comes the discussion of forced learning and accountability. Can we make students learn material that they are not developmentally or experientially ready to learn? Who are we responsible to—the student or the public (which primarily consists of parents, school administrators, and state departments of education)? Should we require students to be held accountable for specific factual information such as math computation facts, or do we train them on how to access the facts when they need them? Would all students want to be readers if we waited for them to pick the time to learn to read? Would it be more beneficial to move from our remedial deficit emphasis educational model to one of investing in student talent and be less concerned with correcting problems? All are questions of priorities and how we invest time and resources.

The students that most often experience great setback from non-depth exploration are the gifted. One important characteristics of gifted learners is that they learn by immersion. They want to know all they possibly can about a given topic of study, and they are not interested in surface information about many different subjects. Once they have the opportunity to reach saturation on a given topic, they want to move on to another area. The frustration they feel when they are constantly moved from subject matter to subject matter throughout the day is astronomical. The easiest way to compensate for the frustration is to stop becoming interested. The turning off of intellectually gifted students is a problem the classrooms must address. Let them do quality work. Grant them time to do, explore, to go into depth, and to become immersed.

I believe not only the gifted, but all children average and the so-called below average want to learn by immersion. It is interesting to watch young children during free play. They engage in an activity, investigate, discuss and then move on to another activity when they sense completion. The completion is the saturation point and it is self-determined. Take any one child and at any given time and his/her attention span will vary based on what he/she is interested in. When allowed the time to explore their interests and accomplish quality work, children perceive themselves as having talent and the process of becoming self-motivated learners begins. It is this process of developing a self belief system which is basic to learning and the emergence of a quality worker.

One of the most fascinating and exciting phenomena to watch is the emergence of a strong, secure, and efficient reader. It can't be forced; it happens as the student investigates, becomes interested, wants more in-depth exposure and immersion, and then perceives self as a reader. Then comes the confidence and willingness to invest the energy to become good at the process. Try to force the process before the student is ready to investigate and become immersed in exploration, and the process is rejected, another poor reader produced. Time is the factor that causes reading failures, not technique, as we will not allow the student the needed time to develop his/her interest. We invest millions of dollars on remediating reading programs that are seldom successful as they emphasize technique, where the real problem is time.

The movement to whole language, the integrated curriculum, manipulation of class schedules into small or large allotments, rearrangement of teaching days into the six day week are examples of trying to more effectively use time and increase learning. All have degrees of success, but have not eliminated the overload of subject matter learning and have not created enough time to learn the subject matter at a quality level.

The issue that must be addressed is not rearranging what already exists, but making decisions on what needs to be removed. This can only happen when teachers themselves are placed in the position of determining what needs to be taught. They are the most qualified to make these decisions. They are the ones doing the teaching and being held accountable for the degree of student learning.

The system, through top down management and its creation of mid managers empowered to create curricula and dictate what is to be taught, has produced classroom expectations which have destroyed quality.

The process to determine what needs to come out of the curriculum to allow indepth quality learning must be reverse from administrative hierarchy decision making to classroom teachers being in charge of what needs to be taught. The teacher needs to work within the school to determine aims and a scope and sequence, but have the freedom to create relevant learning based upon their own interests and the interests of the students in the classroom. The units of study become topical, focus on integration of subjects, and offer the individual learner the opportunity to choose areas of study that are of personal interest and require in-depth, hard work to complete.

Basic information about a given area of study that needs to be understood by everyone in the class is delivered by the teacher. It isn't necessary to test students on basic information as their in-depth investigation and creation of learning products indicate their understanding. It's the creation and demonstration of student-driven learning products that are the significant outcomes that indicate the degree of learning that students are experiencing. District-created curriculum cannot and do not provide learning opportunities for the vast amount of talents, experiences, interests, and energy levels of the individual students in our classrooms.

What is needed is for teachers to have the time necessary to create exciting learning for their students. Instead of mid-level managers, the need to hire additional staff to assist in classroom teaching and free the regular classroom teacher to have the time to do effective planning. Team teaching or floating building classroom teachers can be utilized to satisfy this need.

VERTICAL GROUPING

I have been introduced to a time alternative in Australia, called vertical grouping, that has great potential for increasing quality learning. This process goes beyond tinkering and results in a significant structural change. Vertical grouping is built upon the concept of an integrated age level classroom. It has three age level students stay in a single classroom for three years, with the same teacher, studying the same topics, engaging in the same skill building at the same time. The curriculum becomes a three curriculum: math is a three-year process, reading is a three-year process, etc. As the students engage in study, the products or skill building achievements are based over the three developmental years. In a primary vertical grouped class there would be seven six-year-olds, seven seven-year-olds, and seven eight-year-olds. At the completion of the school year, the seven eight-year-olds would be passed on to fourth grade as we do in traditional horizontal grouped classes, and seven new six-year-olds, ripe out of kindergarten, would enter the class.

Horizontal grouping (our present method of grouping students into a class) has the student placed for nine months (aged same), evaluated at the end of the nine months, and then re-distributed for nine months in a new grade and teacher. The closest arrangement that we presently have to vertical grouping is split grades. However, they are operationally and philosophically very different from vertical grouping.

In split grade grouping we keep separate curriculum in operation and attempt to teach to two different age level groups in the same room. The major purpose for split grades is that we have a certain number of students that don't fit our neat, tightly packaged plan of same age, same curriculum, same number of student sections, same year-after-year material idea of education. When we do split grades, it's to try to figure out how to get through a year and seldom is perceived as a positive model.

Vertical grouping should be used in the lower grades and should be implemented on a teacher/parent choice basis. The schools could have both traditional horizontal grouping consisting of same age students in the same grade, and vertical grouping of multi-age students that stay together as a group for three years. Vertical grouping has definite advantages for quality management and quality work by the students. These advantages will be discussed in the remainder of this chapter.

Skills Acquisition

Acquisition of skills is one of its strong points. The teacher has three years to assist the students in their acquisition of basic academic skills. The major academic skill building for primary students is in reading and math. Precious time is spent in end-of-year closure activities. The beginning of the year requires a significant amount of getting to know the students personally and then determining their skill levels in reading and math so learning activities can be geared to meet specific learner needs. Grouping patterns in reading and math must be established and materials found to meet the unique needs. The end of the academic year requires testing for documentation of academic and social levels of achievement, the recording of the information, and the decision regarding promotion to the next grade. Often there is time spent in meetings to determine the best placement in the new grade. This would be eliminated. The three-year process is continuous. The largest number of new students entering the classroom would be seven or eight. The other sixteen or so would be in place to continue forward with their learning.

Reading and math outcomes would be evaluated over a three-year basis, instead of the horizontal, every nine-month process. The nine-month time limitation of horizontal grouping puts overwhelming pressure on the student and teacher. It is expected that basic reading and math skills are to be completed during the first nine months of school. There is a significant number of students who simply need more time for readiness, and the pressure of nine months' skill attainment is too much for them. As the pressure builds they become the behavior problems. As the pressure to do the work to be a successful learner continues, the young student has to make choices, and there aren't a lot of options: (1) they can continue to try, (2) they can try to design ways to get out of the work, (3) they can begin to guess at answers and develop the attitude of I don't care, (4) they can rebel and stop working. Only choice number one parallels quality work habits, and success is what builds and provides the energy for continual trying, so most choose a combination of two, three, or four. Vertical grouping, with the three-year continuation of learning, addresses the problem of time to do both readiness and develop basic skills in reading and math.

Student and teacher accountability is assessed at the end of the three years. As the pressure of time is removed, the classroom develops a much more relaxed atmosphere. The "hurry up, get it done" attitude diminishes. Students respond by knowing it's all right to investigate, to have time to think, to create, and then become readers and mathematicians when they are developmentally ready to work hard at developing those skills.

Students are continually exposed to peers who are at very different skill levels. As they listen, watch, and experience an atmosphere that allows for these individual differences, students feel comfortable at the level they can best achieve. As they experience the different levels of success, their self confidence builds. They become skill seekers and the process of being successful readers, writers, thinkers, and mathematicians evolves.

In the same way, as the younger students listen to and watch their older peers develop and demonstrate advanced skills, they see the accomplishments and realize the benefits of working hard at skill proficiency and maintenance. The classroom depicts and emulates the profits of working hard at skill building through a peer modeling system. This is a more complete picture than our present horizontal system. In the vertical grouped class the younger students are continually learning skills that they see modeled by the older students. Older students have the opportunities to relearn a skill they may have forgotten when it is being introduced to the younger students.

Noncoercive Management

Vertical grouping, with three years of continuous student/teacher interaction, sets the stage for a noncoercive learning environment. This time span grants freedom for experimentation to find effective learning and management strategies for each student, time to implement them, and then time to profit by their effectiveness. This is particularly true for a student that is choosing not to follow reasonable management strategies, such as classroom procedures for completion of work, attending behaviors, interaction with peers, patterns of movement, time scheduling, and interactions with the teacher. The teacher, after experimenting with various techniques, finally has a significant breakthrough with the student. When this breakthrough finally happens in the horizontal pattern, the nine-month school year is nearly over. The student is to be passed on to another teacher and he/she will more than likely have to repeat the same process the following year.

The time taken for experimentation to become effective with hard to manage students distracts from quality learning. I know this is a major concern for teachers as they often discuss how hard it is to find the keys to unlock responsible behavior. They also express concern for what will happen to these students as they move to the next year's classes.

There are always a certain few students who quickly gain the reputation of "just wait to get this one." They become the focus of discussion in the teacher's lounge, are mentioned at staff meetings, and sometimes discussed at social gatherings. The students' reputations, sometimes through jest and sometimes through serious warnings, spreads and becomes accepted. When the student enters the next grade, the perception of what he/she is like is already established, as well as the planned interaction patterns. The common response of the new teacher is to quickly straighten out this student and get him/her in line (which means get tough), and the power struggle for win or lose between teacher and student is immediately implemented. The student retreats to old behavior and the old behavior repeats itself. These power struggles become more frequent and intense as the student develops his/her self perception as a person who is losing control. The student becomes more of a behavior problem, causing more concentrated effort to get him/her in line.

Vertical grouping eliminates this phenomenon, as the teacher is not passing the problem on to another teacher in nine months. To accomplish all their expectations, teachers are in continuous state of conflict over the dictated expectations of state and local educational boards. A major part of noncoercive management is the message that we will work on this situation until we can find a solution that is acceptable to all. We're not going to give up; we will work it out; and we have three years to do it in. Firmly establishing this behavioral environment during the student's primary school years sets the stage for the rest of his/her school and adult life.

Peer Involvement

Multiple-aged students in the same classroom grant the teacher numerous opportunities for structuring quality learning through the student-helping-student models of peer tutoring and cooperative learning. Each of these models, when implemented correctly, has tremendous impact on student learning and motivation.

I have experienced multi-aged students learning when assisting teachers that were developing cooperative learning skills. An area that has always caused concern is how to effectively develop the cooperative learning program for kindergarten and beginning first grade students. Their social and academic skills make it difficult to effectively program the task group outcomes to a level that creates a quality product. They aren't able to read, so written directions are not an option. They are often distracted due to their short attention spans. Some of them have limited social skill development. These all contribute to the difficulty of obtaining quality work.

I was working with a school where the kindergarten teacher and a second grade teacher had already developed a partial learning program that had the second graders paired with kindergartners and doing some academic work together. We used this model to instigate cooperative learning and the results were amazing.

The second graders could read and had developed beginning writing skills, longer concentration and on-task time, and more self-directed abilities. The kindergartners saw the second graders as older, important people who they admired and wanted to be like. The sense of importance the second graders gained, as leaders by being able to demonstrate their reading, writing, and leadership skills was wonderful to watch. The more they modeled their skills, the greater the admiration of the kindergartners.

The kindergartners developed respect for their second grader partners, and wanted to develop the skills they possessed. The motivation of the kindergartners to learn to read, write, and develop their social skills was always at a high pitch.

They worked in task groups of four: two second graders and two kindergartners. The tasks could be more complex due to the reading level and social maturity of the second graders, and the kindergartners worked hard as they learned the role of resourcer, praiser, thinker, questioner, etc. This is what happens in multi-aged classrooms. Learning is continual, involves student teaching student, younger students modeling older students, and the sense of importance for the older student that comes from being needed and wanted during learning. Peer tutoring, cooperative learning, and companion learning are natural, developmental outcomes.

One of the distinct advantages of vertical grouping is having the older student available to assist the beginning learners. Two significant factors that increase academic learning are the individual student's opportunity to demonstrate his/her achievements and have his/her sense of importance acknowledged. This is what student-to-student learning is all about—empowerment.

One of the breakdowns of our traditional horizontal grouping structure is the lack of opportunity for the learner to have a meaningful audience. One of the reasons that learning is so intense and effective in the performing arts curriculum is that the student knows he or she will be demonstrating the skill to an audience. Vertical grouping allows for a meaningful audience within the room.

I often see teachers attempting to find an audience for their students to demonstrate to, and in most cases it becomes younger students. Third graders are readers to first graders, and as I mentioned before, second graders to kindergartners. The process of older students demonstrating a skill to younger students is beneficial for both, as it creates a sense of accomplishment and importance for the older student and sets the stage for motivation as the younger student attempts to emulate the older.

There is also a need for the younger student to demonstrate his/her skill attainment to the older students, which seldom happens in horizontally grouped classes. The younger student gains in self concept and a sense of importance when they are being recognized by older students, and this reciprocal reinforcement is what the vertically grouped classroom offers. Student-helping-student learning is based upon the opportunity to be involved as someone else is developing or demonstrating a skill. It's the two-way process that has the potential to teach respect and admiration for both students. This is beneficial for the younger student as they attempt to emulate the older student. For it to be of prime importance for the learner, it should be demonstrated to older students. They can then congratulate the student for his or her accomplishments. This can happen naturally in the vertically grouped classroom.

Individual Differences

In the vertically grouped classroom the teacher has no choice but to accept the reality of individual differences as the three distinct age groups force the process. The multi-aged students working on the same skills and topical subjects continually demonstrate different levels of work. This classroom environment eliminates the teacher's concern of "how can I allow for different levels of achievement and still acknowledge the fact that each individual student has done their best, their highest quality work?" The multiaged classroom, due to these distinct age groups, naturally accommodates different levels of work.

During a math class, in which the skill being worked on is addition, some students would be working on learning the names of numbers, some on using numbers to count, some on addition of one column of numbers, and some on two columns. All are working on addition outcomes, but there is complete acceptance of differences.

Teachers, when doing traditional horizontal groupings, manage reading providing different levels of achievement through ability grouping within the class. They normally have three reading groups, but the problem is the same age group has to be separated, and it results in the perception that I'm in the fast, average, or slow group. The multi-age group classroom avoids the problem of fast, average, and slow groups, as the students function on many different levels of achievement based on skill acquisition instead of age sameness and appropriate skill levels groups.

The vertically grouped classroom allows for gifted learners to enter into learning at their own levels and then to continue at a faster pace as they are not held back due to age grouping. They can become models for younger and less able students and be utilized as a helper when there is a need for additional help in student skill development. As they work with younger or less able students, their gifts need not be hidden as they become admired and needed.

The student needing additional time for skill acquisition also has the time factor working for him. He can stay at a more basic level of understanding for longer periods of time without being perceived as inadequate.

Integration Model for Special Needs Students

The vertically grouped classroom, with its opportunities to capitalize on individual difference, is an excellent environment for the inclusion of students with exceptional needs. Only in very extreme cases should cognitive disabled, learning disabled, and behaviorally disabled students need to be referred for exceptional needs education. The classroom promotes and continually adjusts for individual differences. The opportunity to include student-to-student learning and the extended time span of three years provides the classroom teacher with major opportunities for effective management structure.

The Chapter I and exceptional education staff, working in a partnership-ping relationship with the classroom teacher, can effectively adjust and provide a learning program that will meet the needs of all learners.

Quality classroom management that uses vertical grouping has unlimited possibilities for increased social and academic outcomes. It's a major departure from our traditional, fragmented, time controlled system of education, but quality classroom management does dictate major adjustments.

7

Long-Term In-depth
Relationships with Parents

Dr. Deming has proven that if industry wants to produce a quality product, part of the process to do so depends on its ability to obtain quality raw materials. In order to accomplish a guaranteed quality product, raw materials cannot be purchased by low bid competition. In most instances the low bidder has to cut back on some aspect of the product, either in the product itself or in its delivery. Deming advocates replacing low bid competition with the development of long-term in-depth relationships with primary suppliers. This creates a positive relationship between the supplier and buyer which then *equates into* wanting to deliver quality material. If the raw material is less than quality, there is a basis for discussion that opens the way to understandings and upgrading the raw material to a quality level.

This same principle has major implications when we implement quality classroom management and create a quality school. Parents are our primary suppliers. They provide us with the opportunity to be a part of the team that can assist their children to become quality workers. The need to build a strong bond between parents, their children's education, and the school is primary for quality education to happen. The parent-school connectedness is basic to quality education.

Parental involvement in school appears to parallel the experiences they had while they were students. The twenty percent of students that are presently successful in school have parents who had been successful learners and participants while in school. These parents are now the involved ones. They are highly supportive of school, attend the extra curricula events, work on money raisers, attend parent-teacher conferences, and project a positive attitude toward school and learning.

The sixty percent of the students that are indifferent to school have parents who are somewhat supportive of school, but keep their distance. They attend parent-teacher conferences but are not deeply involved or overly concerned about their children's education. As long as the children aren't failing and getting into trouble; school and the home are basically separate. Principals and teachers like to maintain the separateness as it keeps the teaching process independent of interference by parents. The school can call on these parents for specific assistance at special events, such as providing treats for the Halloween party, supervisors on field trips, etc., and the parents respond and feel they are fulfilling the expected school role of involved parent. They come and listen to the teacher at parent-teacher conferences, and support their children if they are participants in special events such as musical concerts, athletic events, drama presentations, etc.

The remaining twenty percent of parents are those whose children don't want to come to school, or when they do come, see school as a place where they don't want to be, and cause problems. As a principal I was often involved with these parents. When I attempted to resolve the students' problems by getting the parents involved, one of three patterns emerged: (1) the parents had not be successful learners when they were students and their sense of failure was transferred to their children's perception of school, (2) they saw school as a place that had little positive or negative affect on their lives and as they assessed the importance of school, they saw it as minimal, or (3) they had negative experiences with teachers and were still carrying around some of the hurt and anger with them. Seldom did I find a student having trouble in school whose parent or parents were successful students and involved when they were in school.

If a parent is negative it is transferred to the student overtly, inadvertently, or both. The student then finds him/herself a compatible, understanding adult when schooling presents aspects of difficulty. This happens often in a student's life as he or she has to work hard to be a successful academic and social learner.

The student without strong parent support will find school a hard place to be. If the parents have already removed school from their quality world, and have negative feelings about school—it becomes easy for the students to follow the same pattern. If the school will recognize this and be ready to invest in parents, both economically and in human resources, the sequence of school failure and drop out will stop perpetuating itself.

It is not easy to help parents change their belief systems about schools from one of being indifferent or negative to being positive. It takes long term, in-depth work which becomes the key to assisting and developing a needed partnership. The quality school has parent inclusion in the school as one of its highest priorities. In order for this in-depth inclusion to be successful, various aspects of the involvement must be carefully planned and assumed by the major players in the process of schooling the student. It cannot be expected that classroom teachers have the major responsibility for parent involvement in the school. The classroom teachers have limited opportunity for parent involvement due to the short time span that they have the student.

The principal and guidance personnel working as a team, the classroom teachers, the individual student, and parents must become the team that is responsible for quality education. The responsibility of each of the school-based groups—the principal/guidance team, classroom teacher responsibility, and student responsibility—will be discussed in detail in this chapter.

PRINCIPAL/GUIDANCE TEAM RESPONSIBILITY

There are three aspects to this team's responsibility. The first is their active planning and implementation of parent education in the school. The second is their role as long-term, contact persons for parents. They become the individual that parents 'hook' onto and feel connected with throughout their children's education at the school. The principal and guidance counselors are constant resources who stay actively involved throughout the students' total school experience. The third responsibility is to provide a place for a parents' lounge where parents can meet, discuss, read, participate in parent programs, and feel secure.

A continual opportunity for parent education is one of the major needs that must be addressed in schools. Quality classrooms cannot exist when the parents are disconnected from the school and are viewed by teachers as having an indifferent or negative attitude about school. The continual theme of "what can you expect, it's all undone when we send the child home" has to change to "How can we expect the child to change when we have no programs to help the parent be more effective and supportive of what the classroom is doing?" Parents must have the opportunity for long-term in-depth training in areas of child development, learning-teaching strategies, communication skills, discipline, understanding the need for cooperative partnershipping between parents and teachers, and, when needed, access to a program to increase their own competence in areas of academic achievement. A second parenting program that is needed is provision for the opportunity for parents to come together and discuss their own concerns regarding reasonable rules, schedules, television watching, and all the every-day requirements of being a parent. School is the logical place for this to happen.

Parent education must have as one of its focuses the building of a knowledge base regarding child development. We teachers forget all the training we had regarding child growth and development: how children develop social and learning skills, how to assess levels of social and academic attainment, and how to talk and manage children to develop self confidence and self management skills. We must also realize that many of our students' parents are distanced from their own families and have no immediate contact to find answers to questions about parenting.

I was invited by a child care center to spend an evening with the parents that sent their children to the center and discuss areas of responsible parenting. The evening's program was designed to be relatively open, encouraging them to discuss areas of parenting that were important to them, and to use me as a "sounding board" for their concerns. Sixteen families were represented for the evening program, and I was surprised at the number of young new parents that were attending. As we began to talk I was surprised by the need of the parents to discuss very basic nurturing and physical needs of their children and to ask the basic how-to questions. It was obvious they had no one to talk to about how to raise their babies. I inquired about this awareness, and they quickly wanted to talk about their sense of aloneness, feelings of frustration and inadequacy, and their need to talk to other parents about child rearing. I then asked them if they have parents or relatives with whom they discussed their concerns of parenting, and I discovered that only three of the sixteen families lived within a close enough proximity to their own families to have the needed contact and support of parents or family.

The principal/guidance parent training team has the responsibility to provide the in-depth training programs to parents on both day and evening schedules.

There are professionally developed parent training programs such as Parent Effective Training, STEP, that can be used, or such programs may be developed by the team. At no time are the educational programs designed for an individual parent to dominate the program and focus only on his or her child. The programs are designed to provide a knowledge base on issues and topics, followed by skill training and then opportunities for application.

Parents also need to get together and discuss everyday parenting concerns. The principal-guidance team would meet this need by scheduling a series of "Parent Discussion Meetings" where the discussion would be topic specific, one session in length and focused around parenting experiences. The discussion formats would be either an open meeting or a motivational meeting, which allows for small group interaction. The group size should not exceed twenty. This opportunity opens possibilities for relationship building between parents and for developing understanding and strategies to meet the continual demands of parenting.

The groups would be formed on the age level of their child or children and have age-level appropriateness as their focus. They would be facilitated by the principal, guidance personnel, and at various times might call upon the classroom teacher as a resource.

The following topics have proven to be effective for parent discussions:

Management
Discipline
Communication (ways to talk with vs. talking to)
Listening skills
Entertainment—quality time
Stories to read to child(ren)
Breaking traditional stereotypes
Getting ready for school
Developmental stages of children (physically and emotionally)
Nutrition
Quality relationships
Expectations and responsibilities
Self-esteem
Resolving conflicts
Coping with stress
Time management
Writing relatives thank you notes
Money—how to earn, shop, spend wisely
Chores: deciding jobs, rotating responsibility
Input for vacation or day off
T.V. watching guidelines for bed time

The second major need for the principal/guidance team is to establish a relationship with the parents that spans the length of time their student attends the school. The parents' opportunity for effective parent training and development of parent discussion groups set the stage for this connection.

One of the frustrations parents talk about is "Who do I go to when I know my child is having problems in school?" There is high probability that the problem is related to the classroom. It often has to do with either peer relationships, teacher personality, or work performance. When the parent contacts the teacher, the results are often the beginning of a power struggle between the teacher and the parent as the teacher personalizes the situation and becomes defensive of his or her position. When the parents can't get what they consider a reasonable understanding or change, they often contact the principal, only to find that the principal supports the teacher. The frustration increases.

The change of role of the principal/guidance team to being the primary connector to the parents changes this scenario. The principal/guidance teams become the starting point for solutions to concerns and problems, and when it is built on long-term in-depth discussions leading to greater understanding, problems have a higher probability of being solved. The team has the opportunity to engage other parents in problem-solving sessions and offer options that lead to solutions.

When the problem has to be dealt with directly, the opportunity for a three-way conference of the parent, teacher, and principal is automatically implemented. The principal is in a position to facilitate the conference and assist both the parent and the teacher to move toward solution.

I remember well the feelings of frustration and resentment toward both the parent and the teacher when, as the principal, I was caught between the two forces. There had already been encounters between the two parties, often without me being informed, and both had become very sure that their position was the correct one. One or the other would contact me expecting that I would defend their positions. When I would meet with the other side, they would try to convince me they were right and expect me to support their position. It was lose/lose for all.

If my position as principal had been established as the primary link for parents to the school, most of the teacher-parent power struggles could have been avoided or professionally and quickly solved. It is imperative in quality managed schools that the initial linkage of parents to school be defined as a principal's responsibility.

The Parent Lounge

As parents become an integral part of the quality school, they will be encouraged to and want to spend more and more time in the school. In order for this to happen they will need a special space for meeting, relating, being involved in parent education, and socializing. This space needs to be primarily for parents, and should not be an area that is shared as part of the teachers' lounge. The school needs to provide a special space that can be developed by the parents as the parent lounge area. The lounge will need to be a pleasant area with comfortable surroundings. It should include a reading area, comfortable moveable furniture that encourages talking and relating to each other, an area for posting articles and notices, and a place for the bottomless cup of coffee.

The lounge area will have multiple use limited only by the creativity of the parents. Basic uses will be for continual in-depth parent training programs, the posting of parent information by teachers, as a repository for reading materials, as a screening room for films showing aspects of child development and teaching techniques, as a platform for special speakers, a space for children's clothes exchange days, a place to just meet and get to know each other, and the many other creative purposes that will evolve.

The lounge must be available for parents whenever school is in session. The cup of coffee, the opportunity for discussion and meeting other parents, the feeling part of the school, and being welcome is continual. A parent volunteer from the various classrooms is always in the lounge to meet and welcome the other parents, to check out reading material, and to serve the cup of coffee.

I had the opportunity to work in a school in Australia, doing inservice work relating to quality management. One of the schools was in the process of developing a parents' lounge. The positiveness of the lounge, even though it was in the beginning stages, was exciting. The teachers were feeling more comfortable with parents and the beginning of partnershipping was emerging. The teachers stated that the idea of the parent lounge was initially frightening and took major readjustment in their thinking. They said that they were concerned about infringement regarding their classroom space and how they taught. They also stated that they thought they would lose, through familiarity, some of the respect of being a teacher. After experiencing the lounge, both of their areas of concern were not warranted and they said it was the best thing that could have happened to the school.

The parents often mentioned their new understanding and appreciation of teachers, as they had the opportunity to be in the school during school hours and see the complexity of managing a school and classroom for quality education. They said they could understand why, at times, a teacher might be short and not ready to communicate with them about their children, as it had to do with exhaustion and frustration. The guidance counselor was the major coordinator and parent educator for the program, and parents often talked of how much they appreciated her services. She was conducting parent education classes, as well as being available for one-on-one conferences when it pertained to assisting the parents with parenting skills.

The last inservice day I conducted was on quality management pertaining to developing a noncoercive environment. The day was designed for both teachers and parents and was very successful.

The day was mandatory for teachers and open to parent participation, and the attendance consisted of three parents for each teacher. The productivity of the day was outstanding. The teachers and parents worked in small groups discussing, planning, and developing specific strategies of how to remove rewards and fear from the classroom and the home. As they discussed and problem solved, I could not differentiate who was teacher and who was parent as respect and in-depth involvement dictated the process.

A quality school will have parents greeting students and their parents when they enter the school grounds before school begins. Parents will be on the playgrounds during recess and noon hours, talking to and assisting students; students will see their parents in the halls during school, and the message will be that working together we can and will have quality education.

TEACHER TO PARENT RESPONSIBILITY

Partnershipping

Parents need to feel welcome and be viewed as a significant part of the school, as co-educators and decision makers regarding their children's education. Quality schools will move the present level of involvement, which is primarily servitude, to in-depth partnershipping. Parents presently are encouraged to participate in occasional school planned social gatherings; attend school special events such as plays, concerts, athletic contest; to volunteer and assist the classroom teacher; to be the classroom representative; to participate in preparation and assisting the classroom teacher for special classroom events such as valentine parties; to act as chaperones for field trips or outdoor educational experiences—primarily experiences that are for the benefit of the school. In-depth parent-school partnership will encourage the parents to participate in a helping relationship with the school but will also include them at a level of decision making that directly affects their children's education.

This transition to parent/teacher partnership will require a change of teacher attitude. Teachers have been encouraged by their profession to set themselves as the expert, which in teaching they are, but have not been encouraged or assisted in knowing how to share this expertise with parents. There is a prevailing attitude among professional school personnel that as the experts we will share what we believe needs to be shared regarding the teaching of your child, when we feel it needs to be shared, most often at parent-teacher conferences or crisis called meetings. Seldom does a parent get an invitation to have a one-on-one meeting with their child's teacher for the sharing of positive experiences. For most parents, when they are called in for a conference, it brings back memories of being called to the principal's office, "I'm in trouble again and wonder what is going to happen to me now."

I have been present when parents have challenged the teacher as to what the child is being taught and/or how the teacher is managing. There is strong teacher support from co-workers and administration that the teacher is justi-fied to teach what curriculum dictates and the right to use the applied teaching techniques they choose. Seldom is the parent seen as a positive force when challenging content or techniques.

Classroom teachers will assume the responsibility of being in constant contact with parents regarding two specific points. Point one is informing the parents of what their children are being taught. Point two is informing the parents of how the units of study are being accomplished and what they can do to assist. The classroom teacher, through continual parent informational meetings and written communications, will inform the parents of units of study that are upcoming as well as specific techniques that will be used in the teaching of the units. As the teacher assumes the role of parent informer regarding specific teaching that is ongoing, the parent has the opportunity to become actively engaged in the process. The information that the parent receives is specific and includes the proposed learner outcomes, the specific teaching techniques that will be employed, the type of evaluation that will be used, the opportunity for in-depth study, and suggestions for the parent/student involvement (Figures 9 and 10).

Parents will be encouraged and be given suggestions as to including complimentary family experiences to encourage their children to have experiences that will coincide with school studies. Trips to the library, museums, parks, short drives, discussions with family members or acquaintances all take on a purpose as the teacher/parent partnershipping begins to have meaning.

The parent information sheet will have a return section that encourages parents to suggest specific learning outcomes that they would like to see included in the units. The parent outcome suggestions can, at times, be incorporated into the general knowledge base of the unit or may be used for specific in-depth exploration through individual or small group work. The opportunity for the parent to have input as to what is being taught is a critical factor to effective parent/teacher partnershipping and quality learning.

Parents who have expertise in special interests in a specific unit of study are encouraged to assist in teaching the unit as co-teachers. The inclusion of the expertise and talents of parents must become an integral part of quality managed classrooms.

As parents sense the wanting of their ideas regarding what is being taught and the inclusion of their interests and talents as part of the teaching process, their importance in their children's education takes on more meaning.

Homework

A second area of teacher responsibility to the parent has to do with homework. The quality managed classroom will have homework defined as work that can only be done at home as it cannot be accomplished in the classroom. When we assign homework that is classroom manageable we create a situation that has great potential for low quality work. Written answers to specific questions, math assignments that are sheets or pages of computation problems, ditto sheets or workbook pages, all work that should be completed in the classroom, seldom is done at home in an attitude that promotes quality work. When I ask students about homework, their perception is that it isn't necessary and/or that it is punishment.

When the students leave school at the end of the day, and having worked hard, they do not take the idea of continuing the work as a pleasant picture. They are wanting to get on with their day. Oftentimes, for the young child, this means some free time at home or in the neighborhood. For middle school

Dear Parents:

This letter is to inform you about beginning the process for a partnership arrangement in the teaching and learning of your child. It is my belief that, in the sharing of the responsibility of teaching, a more quality education will be the outcome. Your insights gained from having raised your child are invaluable in assisting me to understand and more effectively manage the classroom to ensure quality learning.

Any time you feel it necessary for a conference, please contact me and we will set a time to meet and I will do the same with you. I also believe that it is important that your son or daughter also has the right to call a conference that would involve the three of us and whenever a conference is held, your child is always encouraged to attend.

I will be sending an informational form to you that will provide you with the what, why, and how of what will be taught in major units of science and social studies. The form will also update you on what is being emphasized in the reading, language arts, and math areas. The form will be sent to you prior to the beginning of each major teaching unit and as well as providing you with information about the unit, will ask for your suggestions about content, activities that you can do with your child to motivate and assist by home involvement, and provide opportunity for you to participate in classroom activities.

A sample of the informational sheet is included. Please look it over and if you have any questions, contact me.

Sincerely,

Figure 9.   Sample Letter From Classroom Teacher to Parents

learners, some time at friends' homes or time to listen to music. High schoolers need time to go to work to earn spending money. Homework is not what they leave school wanting to do.

The most common pattern for completion of homework is to leave it to the last minute before bedtime. The late afternoon and evening has been spent having fun, energy levels have been depleted, and the evening television shows have appeal, and all of a sudden, it's bedtime and the homework hasn't been done. Hurry up and get it done as quickly as possible or put it off until

UNIT
PRIMARY SUBJECT AREA
DATES OF UNIT
  The unit will be integrating the following subjects:
  ___ physical education
  ___ language arts
  ___ science
  ___ math
  ___ social studies
  ___ art
  ___ music
Projected student outcomes:
  Academic
Social
Classroom Learning Activities
  ___ Individual reading assignment
  ___ Student selected area of in-depth study
  ___ Student selection of a final product that exemplifies quality work
Student participation
  ___ open class meeting
  ___ motivation class meetings
  ___ basic task group work
  ___ cooperative task group work
Home involvement that will enhance your child's learning.
  Suggested activities:
    Discussion areas
    Reading materials
    Field trips
Emphasis areas in Reading/Language Arts
  Math

Please return the following if you are willing to participate in classroom activities or have subject content you would like to have considered as part of the unit.

Specific areas of study that you would like to have considered for inclusion in the unit.

Experiences or professional training that provides you with expertise to share during classroom teaching.

Name: **Date:**

Figure 10. Sample Informational Sheet

morning—this becomes the norm. The idea of doing quality work is totally bypassed, and the product is quickly, sloppily done, so they won't be in trouble the next morning when it is due to be handed in. It reinforces the problem of students doing poor quality work by forcing the ideas of "just get it done and turn it in."

A second pattern for homework completion centers on the plan that the work be completed before any afternoon entertainment can begin. The students view this as punishment because they want to be free to enjoy the late afternoon. The parent, using the student's wanting to have free time, attempts to force the completion of homework, with the student becoming either resentful or quickly getting the work done to have time to do what they want.

Homework places parents into two positions: the enforcer and second teacher. In the role of enforcer there is opposition to the parent when the student is made to do the work, resulting in resentment and anger. The parent is put into the position of attempting to use power to insist the work be done, and the student responds with resistance and conflict follows. In both the immediate after school and late evening model, when the moment comes that the work has to be done, the result is avoidance either by direct conflict or stalling. When the work is finally forced to be done, low quality work is the outcome.

When the parent is placed in second teacher position, conflict also emerges. Teacher expectancy of homework is that the work is completed and the parent is to assist when the student is experiencing difficulty with the content. The student already has a feeling of resentment about having to do the homework, and this low-level anger is projected toward the parent who is to be in the helper role. The process dictates incompatible roles: enforcer vs. helper.

There are many areas where, in the teaching of subject matter, the parent is incapable. The subject matter may be too complex, or the parent attempts to teach as they were taught and techniques have significantly changed, causing major confusion on the part of the student. The result is the student feels the parent is incompetent and disaster follows.

A single parent gave the following account of her dilemma with homework. She finished work at five and then had to go to the day care center to pick up her three elementary-aged children. When she got home, after working eight hours, she just wanted to have fun and relax with her family. Her third grade daughter had a teacher who believed in homework and viewed it as an every day extension of the classroom. The daughter was struggling with math, so it became the subject matter for homework. Every night the same ordeal took place: first a series of behaviors to try to avoid the dilemma of struggling with math, followed by refusal to work, followed by anger toward mom, and then the confusion of mom trying to explain third grade math (as she had been taught) to her daughter (who was being taught very differently). By the time the evening was over everyone was angry, and everyone more resentful toward the school. Not only was quality work deteriorating, so was quality parenting.

Quality managed classrooms will change significantly as the teachers consistently communicate to the parent what is being taught, how it is being taught, and how the parent can become meaningfully involved. Students will understand that hard work is part of the school day, and that it is to be completed during the school day. As the students set their high standards of work they will also be learning how to set time allotments to finish the work. In the process of setting time standards, they may choose to do some outside research that will include work outside the classroom. This student selected outside school work as what will replace traditional homework.

Homework will become work that can not be done in the school as it will require resources that are not available in the schools. It will focus on discussions with people, interviews, viewing special television shows for information or analysis, use of public library, visits to art museums, attendance of plays, concerts, athletic events, etc., limited only by the creativity of the student and the teacher. As the parent is informed about the units of study, the parent is provided with suggested activities that can be used to assist their students' learning. The activities focus on the inclusion of resources that are in the home or community.

The natural inclusion of parents is in the areas of their children's discussion with them what they are learning, and providing experience that will enhance the learning that cannot be done at school.

STUDENT-LEAD PARENT CONFERENCES

The third major change of long term in-depth parent relationships has to do with redefining student responsibility to the parent. The quality managed classroom is continually controlling for ways to have the individual student take ownership of his/her learning and to have a meaningful audience to demonstrate their competencies to. One of the main reasons that extra curricular events have a high degree of relevancy is the fact that there is an audience to demonstrate competency too. The musician, athlete, and actor all work hard as they know they will need to be outstanding during the performance. Traditional academic classroom learning has never created this opportunity for performance.

A major shift of parent involvement is the replacement of traditional parent-teacher conferences with student-parent conferences. Kindergarten through second grade will be three-way conferences of student, parent, and teacher. The teacher will play less of a dominant role as communicator as the student progresses through second grade. From third grade on the student will conduct the conference on an individual basis. The conference provides the student with the continual need to take ownership of their learning as they assess and collect relevant material for the conference. The conference then becomes the means of reporting and demonstrating the significant accomplishments.

Traditional parent-teacher conferences, which are usually accompanied by early student release days or a non-attending student day, are tightly scheduled, exhaustive, require a high degree of teacher planning, and primarily provide the parent with information that has little impact upon the motivations and learning outcomes of the student. The student is being reported on, and as such has minimal direct control over what to do to influence the conference, and in most instances, either waits with great apprehension for his/her parent to come home to find out the results of the conference, or pays no attention to the process. When I was teaching upper elementary age students I would ask them what their parents thought about the conferences and many of them would answer by telling me they didn't know!

The student-led conference is designed as a highly motivational technique and places the student in a position of direct responsibility as to what the content of the conference will be. The student, independent of the teacher, has the opportunity to report on his/her accomplishments, units of study that have been of importance to him/her, areas that require extra effort, future plans pertaining to study areas, extra curricular interest and participation, and the opportunity to demonstrate a sense of ownership of his/her classroom by showing the parents around the room, to take their parents to special interest areas in the school such as the IMC, computer room, art and music rooms, and to introduce the parent to their teacher and principal (Figure 11).

The students, through the creation of their conferencing portfolios, are constantly aware of the need to assess their work and collect samples that

PHASE I
(5 minutes)
Introduction of parent to teacher, conference purpose, and procedure.
- Parent is introduced to teacher
- Student and parent proceed to assigned area for conference
- Student, utilizing a pre-developed plan for conference, explains purpose of conference and the sequence that will be used

Purpose
1. To welcome and acquaint parent with their room and school
2. To discuss with parent what she/he is studying
3. To answer questions the parent has about what is being studied
4. To present evidence of what she/he is learning
   - present samples of work in each subject area
   - discuss assessment portfolios
5. To demonstrate skills she/he has learned

PHASE III
(15 minutes)
Discussion of the special pullout program areas
- art
- music
- hysical education
- computer room
- learning media center

Student highlights projects, units, outcomes in the special areas
1. selects experiences where she/he has experienced success
2. discusses the experiences and, when possible, shows evidence of learning

PHASE II
(40 minutes)
Systematic presentation of accomplishments regarding academic learning
1. Subject
2. Areas of study
3. What she/he has learned
4. Examples of work that validate the learning—portfolio or file of accomplishments
5. When appropriate, demonstration of skill competencies
   a. reading-language arts
   b. math
   c. science
   d. social studies

The student proceeds through each of the four areas.

PHASE IV

Tour of the building, emphasizing the specialty areas, time spent showing special aspects of the special area, introduction of parent to special area teacher, ending in the principal's office area.
1. Introduction of parent to principal
2. Coffee, tea, juice, and cookies

This format will be used for the fall conference. Spring conference will utilize only Phases I, II, and III.

Figure 11. Student-Led Parent Conference

exemplify what they want to report to their parents. This need for continual self assessment is basic to their doing quality work. The work takes on a significant purpose when they realize they are going to be able to share it with someone of importance. The ongoing self assessment and collections also make a realistic situation for the teachers to discuss with the student what is important in school and assist them in the process of creating the portfolios.

The teachers also have the responsibility to teach the students the process of conferencing. The progression of the conference must be explained, demonstrated, and then practiced in role play by the students. They need to be taught that introductions take place first, followed by an explanation of the purpose of the conference, an overview, specific subject matter discussion with work samples that demonstrate work done, demonstration of competence, and if a student chooses, a tour of the school.

The conference should be about an hour in length, and have four scheduled at the same time. The four individual conferences are accomplished in assigned areas of the room, and the teacher is present at all times. She/he, after having been introduced to the parents circulates from conference to conference, monitoring the process to assure that the conference plan is being followed and that specific material and competencies are covered. During the process of circulation, the teacher will need to have self discipline to refrain from becoming directly involved in the conference.

As students become skilled at parent conferencing the conferences will replace the common report card system of reporting. We all know that grading is one of the biggest headaches and farces in education. The common report card, be it "A-B-C" or any of the other configurations of A-B-C, seldom reports a students potential for learning, or how much she/he actually knows, or can do. Student-parent conferencing is an alternative to report cards. As the student begins to control for quality as part of their learning and learns the process of self-assessment, individual grade assessment becomes a negotiated compromise between the student and the teacher. The student then assumes the responsibility to report his/her grade to the parent during parent-student conferences and has the opportunity to demonstrate competence to verify the grade. These student-parent conferences will need to be scheduled three times throughout the academic year.

In a quality managed classroom it is understood that along with scheduled student-parent conferencing the parent, teacher, or student can call a conference of a specific purpose at any time. Being that the conference has as its focus the students interest, the student is always actively involved in the conference. The student is always informed of the conference, by the parent or teacher, when ever one initiates the requests, and assistance and time is provided to give the student the opportunity to prepare for the conference. The student is always present and encouraged to participate.

The parent-teacher partnership is built upon open communication, trust, and respect. As the three areas of principal/guidance team, teacher, and student responsibility become defined, developed, and implemented, the parent role of partner becomes solidified. Quality learning is the outcome.

Bibliography

American Association of School Administrators. (1991). *An introduction to total quality for schools: A collection of articles on the concepts of total quality management and W. Edwards Deming.* Arlington, VA: Author.

American Association of School Administrators. (1994). *Quality goes to school: Readings on quality management in education.* Arlington, VA: Author.

Bonstingl, J. (1992). *Schools of quality: An introduction to total quality management.* Alexandria, VA: Association for Supervision and Curriculum.

Byrnes, M., Cornesky, R., & Byrnes, L. (Eds.). (1992). *The quality teacher: Implementing total quality management in the classroom.* Bunnell, FL: Cornesky & Associates.

Deming, W. (1993). *New economics for industry, education, government.* Cambridge, MA: MIT.

Deming, W. (1986). *Out of the crisis.* Cambridge, MA: MIT.

English, F. (1994). *Total quality education: Transforming schools into learning.* Newbury Park, CA: Corwin Press, Inc.

Fields, J. (1993). *Total quality for school: A suggestion for American education.* Milwaukee, WI: ASQC Quality Press.

Glasser, W. (1969). *Schools without failure.* New York: Harper Collins.

Glasser, W. (1986). *Control theory in the classroom.* New York: Harper Collins.

Glasser, W. (1992). *The quality school.* New York: Harper Collins.

Glasser, W. (1993). *The quality school teacher.* New York: Harper Collins.

Johnson, D., Johnson, R., & Johnson-Holubee, E. (1992). *Advanced cooperative learning.* Edina, MN: Interaction Book Company.

Johnson, D., Johnson, R., & Johnson-Holubee, E.J. (1990). *Circles of learning: cooperations in the classroom* (3rd ed.). Edina, MN: Interaction Book Company.

Johnson, D., & Johnson, R. (1989). *Leading the cooperative school.* Edina, MN: Interaction Book Company.

Kaufman, R. (1992). *Mapping educational success: Strategic thinking and planning for school administrators.* Newbury Park, CA: Corwin Press, Inc.

137

Kohn, A. (1992). *No contest: The case against competition* (rev. ed.). New York: Houghton Mifflin.

McGinnis, E., & Goldstein A. (1984). *Skillstreaming the elementary school child: a guide for teaching prosocial skills.* RES Press.

McGonagill, G. (1992). *Overcoming barriers to educational restructuring.* Arlington, VA: American Association of School Administrators.

Savary, L. (1992). *Creating quality schools.* Arlington, VA: American Association of School Administrators.

Scheetz, M. (1994) *Developing total quality education: A view from the inside.* Newbury Park, CA: Corwin Press, Inc.

Scherkenbach, W. (1991). *Deming's road to continual improvement.* Knoxville, TN: SPC, Press, Inc.

Scherkenbach, W. (1991). *The Deming route to quality and productivity.* Washington, DC: CEEP Press.

Walton, M. (1989). *The Deming management method.* New York: Perigree Books.

www.ingramcontent.com/pod-product-compliance
Ingram Content Group UK Ltd.
Pitfield, Milton Keynes, MK11 3LW, UK
UKHW020348010325
455677UK00021B/349